joy *will* come

EXCHANGE SHAME
FOR REDEMPTION

joy *will* come

EXCHANGE SHAME
FOR REDEMPTION

Lindsay Pepin Ophus with
Scarlet Pepin and **Bethany Pepin**

HONOR✠NET
PUBLISHERS
Sapulpa, OK

Joy Will Come
ISBN 978-1-938021-46-6

Copyright © 2019 by
Lindsay Pepin Ophus
with Scarlet Pepin and Bethany Pepin

Published by HonorNet Publishers

P. O. Box 910
Sapulpa, OK 74067
Website: honornet.net

CONTENTS

INTRODUCTION

This is a book about redemption, about healing, and about life change through Christ.

This book is for the broken. It is for those who feel too far gone. You cannot outrun Christ's love. You cannot mess up too much. There is hope.

This book is for the girls who are secretly having sex. You have value. You are not dirty. You are still wanted and loved by your Heavenly Father.

This book is for the unplanned pregnancy. Your baby is not a sin. You do not have to live in shame. Your baby is a gift from God. You have options. There can be life after this pain.

This book is for the family or the friends of someone who is hurting or lost. Their life choices are not your fault. You can show Christ's love in your actions every day. You can support them in a healthy way.

This book is for the people who were placed for adoption. Your mother loved you more than you will ever know. Your mother loved you so much she wanted to give you the best life possible. You are not a mistake. You were always wanted. You are a child of God.

This book is for the babies who did not get to breathe on earth. May your death not be forgotten. May the Lord heal the women who aborted you, and may your life in the womb be an encouragement to others that there are other options.

Lindsay Pepin Ophus

CHAPTER 1

Lindsay

THE TEST IS POSITIVE. YOU'RE PREGNANT.

I was stunned. As a senior in high school I was used to hearing words like, "Congratulations!" or "Way to go; you've made it!" But never, "You're pregnant." That's why I was totally unprepared when the nurse at the Planned Parenthood Clinic gave me the news.

I immediately went into shock, and my brain seemed to disconnect from reality. I couldn't feel a thing. All I could do was look at the ugly brown cabinets in the tiny, stifling exam room. I could hear that she was still talking to me, but all I could do was stare blankly at those cabinets. I couldn't even focus on what the woman was trying to tell me. All I could think about were those ugly brown cabinets.

I remember the nurse standing on my right side. Bryan, my boyfriend, was standing on my left. The nurse just kept droning on and on while handing me a never-ending pile of papers, brochures, fliers, and cards. I grabbed each paper and mindlessly set them on my lap. Those brown cabinets were the only thing my mind was able to process. She went on and on about the options for me to consider. But I couldn't comprehend what she was saying. It was way too much information for me to absorb.

The woman finally stopped talking, and I took that as my cue to get up and leave. I gathered up all the papers and brochures and walked like a zombie to the exam room door not saying a word, not to her, not to Bryan. I must've been moving pretty slowly because I can still remember Bryan saying, "Just make it to the main door. Just make it to the main door."

My perfect life, my bright future was now reduced to putting one foot in front of the other just to make it twenty feet out of the clinic. I could feel Bryan's hand on my back gently pushing me forward.

Once outside, the goal became making it to the car. Tears started streaming down my face. These were not tears of sadness or anger but tears of emptiness and helplessness. This might have been the first situation in my life that I wasn't able to control. I simply didn't know what to do but cry. I didn't know how to feel. My body and my emotions were on overload. All I could feel was shock, pure "stop-you-dead-in-your-tracks" shock. My mind was unable to wrap around the fact that I was pregnant.

The Perfect Pepins

Your senior year of high school is supposed to be a time of excitement. There's a reason why everyone cheers when people yell "Seniors"! After twelve years of hard work, there's even a sense of cockiness about your accomplishment. You feel invincible and perfect and you're confident that you're the envy of everyone you pass in the hallway between classes.

Well, at least that's how you're supposed to feel.

Until that day in the clinic, that's the way I felt. I was on top of the world. I was 18, a senior at a huge school with over 700 students in my graduating class. I was competing in pageants, I was on the Student Council, and had been the class president twice during my school years.

Yes, in my own mind, I was the best there was. I was living the life others just dreamed of. I was living life my way. Now, looking back it's easy to see that my pride and immaturity were leading me down the wrong path. But I was convinced that nothing could stop me. I knew that this was going to be my best year yet. I had dreams of attending a Christian college in the fall with the goal of becoming a news anchor after graduating. I loved my life. Things were perfect.

I come from a family with a very strong faith. I've been a Christian since I was three years old. I attended church and youth group regularly, I'd been on two mission trips, and would gladly tell anyone that I loved God with all my heart. Overall, most of the students I knew considered me a good person; some might have even considered me a great person. But the problem was, I was carrying a secret.

I never drank or did drugs. I had a 3.8 GPA. I held myself to a high standard. In my opinion, I thought I was a pretty great Christian kid, except of course for the fact I was sleeping with my boyfriend, a fact I kept hidden from everyone except a couple of my closest friends. I always said that sex before marriage was something I would never do. I'd lie or play dumb if someone confronted me on the issue.

After all, I was a good Christian and Christians don't sleep with their boyfriends. And if they do, they certainly don't go around talking about it. I was haunted by the lies of the enemy (Satan), "You've got to keep this terrible thing a secret. No one can know you're struggling with this. You have a reputation to protect. You are a Pepin, and the "Perfect Pepins" don't mess up!"

But the problem with secrets is that they can eat you alive. Secrets cause you to put on a false front on the outside, faking that everything is just fine, while you are slowly drowning on the inside. Secrets cause you to change your identity, making you believe that all you are is a fraud. To everyone around me, it looked like I had my life together, always laughing, without a care in the world. But when the noise settled and the laughter stopped, I was all alone with my secret … wishing for a way out.

The truth is, I was exhausted. Living a lie is hard work. Always covering, always making sure the lie is kept hidden from others, and doing my best to keep the "Christian" mask firmly in place. I couldn't risk the vulnerability that would come with being honest with those who loved me.

The problem is that the longer you keep the lie alive, the more powerful it becomes … the harder it is to finally come clean. There is a verse in the Bible that says, "…surely your sin will find you out" (Numbers 32:23 NKJV). That's so true. Sin, like a splinter in your finger, is always pushing its way to the surface. In my case, I was in so much denial that I figured if I could keep my sin in secret, no one would get hurt. I believed the lie that I could play around with my sin and not have to suffer the consequences.

We all think we can control our sin. We justify it, telling ourselves that as long as we can keep our sin a secret or as long as we're not hurting anybody, it'll be okay. I was so self-centered I thought I could control my sin, that I could sin on my own terms and I could handle it. Ultimately, my sin found its way to the surface, and I was going to have to deal with it whether I wanted to or not.

Living Up to a High Standard

My family is a unique breed. We are a tight knit group. I have an older sister and a younger sister, and yes, I have always struggled with a massive "middle child syndrome."

At the time, our parents had been happily married for 21 years. My dad is the kind of man that other men look up to and respect. He always wears an ironed shirt, tailored pants, and his hair is perfectly in place. He's a very nice man, slow to anger but strong in his opinions. He made sure that we were honorable, respectful, and an asset to society, and that we knew exactly what was expected of us.

When I was in about the fifth grade, my dad created a chart detailing the things we had to do each day to help with the family and the home. The list on the chart consisted of daily prayer time, exercise, and various chores. On Sunday, we each had an extra item on our to-do list. We had to say at least one thing nice to our sisters. When we completed an item, we were able to put a checkmark next to it on the chart. With each checkmark, we earned a prize. In those days, my dad was a checkmark kind of guy. In my mind, a checkmark on the chart meant that we had his attention and approval. To us, the chart was a fun exercise and we loved earning the prizes. But for my dad, the chart was a valuable learning tool, teaching us to be well-rounded, responsible, and diligent.

Was my dad harsh? No. Never. No matter what, I always knew he loved me and would do anything for his family. I knew that he would be there every morning to wake us up and every night to tuck us in. He coached our basketball teams, joined us on mission trips, and never missed a school program. He was generous, always giving to anyone in need. I never questioned his love for me, but my dad set a very high standard, and I often felt that I had to be on my best behavior to get his approval. But all things considered, my dad was the best human father I could've ever asked for.

My mom is a very different person than my dad … but she's just as intense in her own way. She constantly worried about what other people thought about us and about the impression we were making on them.

This trait was most evident whenever she was going to be hosting an event. My mom is extremely creative and fun to be around, but anytime people were scheduled to come to our home, she was strictly business. "Chore Time" for us always started about four hours before "Party Time."

Whenever it was just my mom and I, we would laugh and laugh. We are very similar and cut from the same fun-loving bolt of cloth. She's the one who always taught me to laugh at myself and enjoy life. She was the best stay-at-home mom who always made sure we had everything we needed and were well taken care of, whether that was elaborate school play costumes or amazingly fun birthday parties. We never wanted for anything.

Perfectly Presented

My parents are not your average people. Their personal relationship with God is something most people would never understand. For my whole life, they put a lot of effort into listening for direction from the Lord, and they always strived to obey Him. They were the poster parents for raising a family in the "perfect" Christian way.

We were constantly being presented as this perfect Christian family. Don't get me wrong; we were a pretty awesome family. All five of us genuinely loved Christ and wanted to follow Him. We also genuinely loved each other, and we would do anything for each other. But to me in my limited perception, there seemed to be an expectation to be perfect and not make a mistake, often at the cost of just being real.

In my young, 18-year-old mind, "perfection" was tied to God's love and acceptance. I had trouble believing that God didn't have some kind of chart of His own, and He was disappointed when I didn't get all the checkmarks I was supposed to be getting. I mistakenly thought that His love for me was determined by the checkmarks I earned.

I thought that striving for perfection was a sign of how much I loved God and wanted to serve Him. I thought that if I could just be perfect, in every way, then He would love me more and He would accept me.

Sadly, I didn't realize that God was never after perfection. He has no chart and He's not after checkmarks. He's after my heart. I love what Rick

Warren says, "God will never love you more or less than He does right now." No matter what you do ... or what you don't do, God's love for you is complete.

But as a teenager, I didn't know that. I didn't even know who I was and found that the weight of perfection was too heavy for me to carry. I mean, I loved Jesus. I really did. I've loved Him since I was a little girl, and I love Him to this day. I always felt that He loved me too. But just like with my earthly father, I often felt like I had to be perfect and earn all my checkmarks in order to earn His attention. But that was only half the equation.

Trying to earn the approval of other people is the other half. Feeling the pressure to live up to the unreasonable expectations of others can be exhausting and impossible. I didn't believe Jesus would fully accept me until I was perfect and whole. I didn't believe He wanted my mess at the foot of the cross.

I often had to recite to myself Romans 8:39: "Neither height nor depth, nor anything else in all creation, will be able to separate us from the love of God that is in Christ Jesus our Lord." No matter how many times I said that verse, I always had trouble believing it. I believed I wasn't perfect enough for the perfect love of Christ. But the truth is, none of us are perfect enough to deserve God's love. That's what grace is all about. God's love for us is so great that it covers our sin no matter how terrible that sin might be. God loves us no matter what, and He is always ready to forgive us when we fall short.

I wish I could go back to teenager Lindsay and remind her to believe every single word of that verse. I wish I could simply hand her the gift of unconditional love, the gift that she had already received through what Jesus did on the cross. It's easy for me to see now that teenager Lindsay never learned how to take hold of the truth revealed in that verse. There was no chart, no box, and no checkmark that would show that she had received that love.

CHAPTER 2

Lindsay

MY LIFE WITH BRYAN

My relationship with Bryan was intoxicating. I was addicted to the love and attention he showed me, and I longed to be with him all the time. I allowed my relationship with Bryan to determine all my emotions. If the relationship was going well, I was upbeat and happy, on top of the world. If things were going bad with him, then I was down and depressed. Instead of Jesus being the center of things, my entire world revolved around my relationship with Bryan. Obviously, I was looking to Bryan to provide those things that only Jesus could give me. Things like unconditional love, acceptance, value, and a positive self-esteem.

By the time our senior year rolled around, Bryan and I were once again wrapped up in our relationship that had been developing on and off since we were both in the eighth grade.

Just like it seemed with everyone else in my life, Bryan had expectations of me.. But I believed Bryan loved me. At the time, I felt like I had no one else in my life who loved me like he did.

But everyone says that, right? My young naïve mind couldn't conceive what true love was. I just assumed I was experiencing true love because I'd never allowed myself to experience the perfect love of Jesus. With every type of human love I had in my life, I sometimes felt the pressure to perform and to be perfect. I was convinced that I had to hit all the checkmarks to get the approval I so desperately desired. Even though Bryan was not always the one who initiated, sex with Bryan left me hating myself … every single time. Shame became my constant companion, and I couldn't shake free.

I once heard that guilt is what you feel when you believe that you are a good person but have done something bad. Shame, on the other hand, is far more damaging. Shame is what you feel when you believe that you are a bad person and can't help doing bad things.

That was exactly how I felt. I might have been perfect on the outside, but it was all a lie. I was deeply flawed. I was disobeying God by having sex with Bryan outside of marriage, and it was so terrible and ugly to me that I couldn't risk seeking help by exposing it. I had to hide it … even from those who loved me most.

The grief I felt from my sin was overpowering. After being with Bryan, I wanted nothing more than to escape to my own bedroom and cry myself to sleep. But whenever I got home around my parents and sisters, my grief would be swallowed up in the shame. I knew I was going against my beliefs and convictions, but I felt helpless to stop. There was something inside of me that just couldn't say no to Bryan.

I wish now that I would've had the courage to ask for help. As teenagers, "help" is a taboo word. But asking for help should never be thought of as taboo. Asking for help needs to be normal for all of us, no matter what stage of life we are in. Help from our families, help from our churches, help from our friends.

If you think about it, help is a natural, instinctive thing to ask for. You don't have to teach a toddler to ask for help. If they can't do something, they will immediately cry out or look to their parents or someone they trust to help them get what they need. So if it's instinctive to little ones, why isn't it instinctive when we get older?

I think it's all a matter of trust. Often, we've been hurt by those we've trusted and as a protection against that, we've made a decision at some point not to trust anymore. We don't trust others with our pain, or our frustration, or with our sin. We simply don't believe that they won't hurt us if they knew our secrets. Of course, all this fits into the strategy the enemy has against us. He wants us to carry our secret burden all by ourselves. He wants nothing more than to keep us from asking for help because he knows that just the act of asking can bring us freedom in such a strong and healthy way.

During my senior year in high school, it seemed like I spent every Sunday in church crying out to the Lord and begging for His forgiveness. I begged Him to take the desire to be with Bryan away. I wanted Him to cleanse me, but I never trusted Him enough to do anything to change my behavior. I kept stepping out of God's will and out from under His protection. While the shame continued to haunt me, the pain from my sin actually seemed to start fading away. Like with every other sin, the more we nurture it, the less it convicts us. We become hardened to it. I was numb and unable to listen to that still small voice of the Holy Spirit in my heart. I justified my sexual relationship with Bryan by telling myself that he was the only source of love in my life, which was a lie.

I was no longer listening to the truthful words of my Heavenly Father. My new truth was that I had to meet an expectation in order to receive love and acceptance. I wonder how often we allow the voices of others to become our voice of truth.

But I thought God didn't even want to talk to me. I believed the lie that I was unable to hear Him. I thought my sin had closed me off to the sound of His voice. I needed to hear the promise from John 10:27 ESV:

"My sheep hear my voice, and I know them, and they follow me." The problem was I was listening to the wrong voice. God was speaking truth to me, but I wasn't listening to Him.

Where Are the Parents?

The truth is … my parents were right there next to me all along. I had listened to the "purity talk" over a thousand times. I sat through countless church services where the pastor went on and on about staying pure. I had heard it so many times, it sounded like a cliché to me. My parents were vigilant, constantly asking me if I was making good choices. My mom worried about me all the time. Her worrying began to annoy me on the one hand and made me feel guilty on the other. Because of this I felt like I couldn't go to her with my secret. I couldn't imagine talking to her about my sexual relationship with Bryan. I knew she would go crazy if she found out. In my view, her fear and anxiety were like a wall that cut me off from her; I felt that there was no way I could go to her for help.

Whenever I came home from spending time with Bryan, I'd try to make it to my room without being caught by Mom with her laundry list of questions. She would ask what Bryan and I did that night and I'd give her the scripted answer, leaving out some key details. I got used to the bitter taste of those lies in my mouth, but those lies kept my parents in the dark. They were completely oblivious to the fact that I was having sex with Bryan. They trusted me and assumed I was busy upholding the image of the perfect Pepin family.

My parents may not have known about Bryan and I having sex, but their parental radar was fully functional; they worried about my relationship with Bryan. We dated on and off all through high school. But no matter how many times we broke up, we never stayed apart very long because we were in the same circle of friends. It seemed like we were always being thrown together. Even though we'd date other people from time to time, we were always drawn back together.

Once we started officially "dating," things got toxic right off the bat. We quickly made each other the main focus of our lives, which is never a good idea. Our relationship became all consuming. We were not only in love with each other; we were best friends, which can be a good thing. But in our case, we had made each other the lord of our lives.

When I was with Bryan, there was no room for God, my friends, or my family … I was always with Bryan. This seems to be a common theme in teenage relationships. Looking back, I wish I would have listened to my parents. Their years of walking with the Lord had put their wisdom decades ahead of mine.

CHAPTER 3

Lindsay

MY NAÏVE PHASE

t's safe to say that December 2011 was undoubtedly the worst month of my life. Well, technically, it actually started the last week of November because something that was supposed to happen didn't happen. I was late.

In the back of my mind, I thought that maybe there was a chance I could be pregnant, but at the same time, I told myself that it could never happen to me. Remember, I thought I could do what I wanted and the consequences that happened to others wouldn't happen to me. Besides, my life was already charted out. I had a plan and I was prideful enough to believe that nothing could change that.

Taking the Test

Then on November 30, ironically right after attending the Fellowship of Christian Athletes (FCA) meeting, Bryan and I went to Walmart and bought a 2-pack of pregnancy tests. Even as I grabbed the tests from the shelf, I wasn't too worried. I mean, why would I get pregnant? My main concern that night was that I would run into someone I knew and they would see me with a pregnancy test. Now that would be awkward!

I took the first test that night in a nasty gas station bathroom while Bryan sat waiting in the car. I walked the stick out to his car, and we waited the three minutes it was supposed to take. The test was negative! Talk about being relieved! We just assumed my period was late because of all the stress I had been experiencing. I felt so much better.

On the way to my best friend Rachel's house, I asked Bryan, "What would we do if I really was pregnant?" He quickly told me, "I would marry you." That was the end of the conversation, but his words would haunt me for the next year.

I carried on with the rest of my week just like everything was normal. I was back on top and in control. It was a close call, but we made it. Nothing could go wrong. Sure, we had sex together, but we used condoms. The pregnancy scare was just a minor bump in the road, no big deal, nothing to freak out about.

That Sunday, Bryan got a call from a college out of state saying that they wanted him to make an official visit to the school. I was excited for him. I knew that as soon as we went to college, we'd be going our separate ways anyway. Sure, I'd be sad when he left, but we both had huge adventures ahead of us.

There was still a problem though. I was now almost two weeks late on my period. After a babysitting job, I went to Bryan's house to celebrate his college news. I had it in my mind to take the other test from the 2-pack, which was still out in Bryan's car.

It was just Bryan and his dad at home so Bryan and I headed upstairs, and I took the test in the guest bathroom. As I'm peeing on the stick, it's already making the plus sign! There was no three-minute wait this time, no gradual fading in. This time it was positive instantly! I couldn't take my eyes off that plus sign. I just set the stick on the counter next to the sink. I convinced myself that if I waited the three minutes, it would change back to a minus sign and we'd be okay. I had zero emotions at the time because, after all, the test had to be wrong. I had no capacity in my mind to think otherwise.

As I started to wash my hands, Bryan came into the bathroom and saw the test on the counter. He was shocked to say the least. We went into the game room, and he started to pace the floor.

My Naïve Phase

I told him to have a seat and calm down. At this point, I hadn't even processed any of this. I still had no emotions about any of it. All I could think of was that his dad was going to overhear us. Bryan finally sat down and I told him, "This isn't over. That test has been sitting in your car in 30-degree weather for five days by now. I'm sure something's not right; it was positive too fast. I know we have options here. I know we can figure something out. There's always adoption, our parents could help out, or we could get married. Bryan, this isn't over; we don't even know whether I'm pregnant or not for sure." I spouted out these facts as if I were a completely unaffected third person. I couldn't be pregnant. This wasn't part of my plan so it must be wrong.

My deep, dark secret was trying to get out; and I was desperately trying to keep it hidden. My perfect life was not suited to this kind of thing. All my plans, and more importantly, all the allusions I'd built up about myself and my life would come crashing down if this secret became known to others. I was in full-on damage control mode.

It's amazing how we can make a plan and have an image of ourselves five or ten years into the future, and we're naïve enough to think that nothing can rock that perfect plan … not even a positive pregnancy test. We create this imaginary bubble of plans and are completely closed off to the realities that might be down the path. Sometimes the plan is interrupted by something wonderful, but other times it is interrupted by something earth-shattering.

What if we are so focused on the plan that we miss the power and purpose Christ has for us? What if something earth-shattering turns into something wonderful? There's a great story in the Bible in John 11. One of Jesus' best friends was sick. His name was Lazarus. Jesus was out of town and couldn't come immediately to pray for His friend, and by the time Jesus could get there, Lazarus had died. His two sisters, Mary and Martha, were crushed. Their lives, which were going along according to plan, had just been turned upside down. Of all the things they'd planned for, I'm sure their brother dying wasn't one of them. They thought they knew the future, but their brother's death had shattered their plans.

But Jesus wasn't rocked. He wasn't surprised or shocked. In fact, there are many who believe that Jesus purposely delayed His arrival. He wanted the opportunity to pray, not just for Lazarus's healing, but for his resurrection. Ultimately, Lazarus was raised from the dead, and it brought even greater glory to God. Mary and Martha almost missed this beautiful miracle. They could've shut down, closing themselves off to what God wanted to do, but instead they chose to trust that Jesus could do what He promised He could do.

But I wasn't thinking about the story of Lazarus and Jesus at the time. All I could think about was my own plan for my life and how that plan did not include a pregnancy.

After Bryan stopped pacing, we sat together on the sofa in silence. Our situation settled around me, and I started to softly cry, not so much because I was pregnant but because of the fear of the unknown. My curfew came around and I left. We told each other we'd figure it out the next day.

I slept fine that night. After all, I was sure that the test was wrong. I mean, I'm a Pepin; these things don't happen to the Pepins. In a perfect world, no one has sex before marriage, and of course, no one ends up pregnant. This is just one big mix-up. The test was in a car where the temperature was below freezing for several cold December days and nights. There's no way it could read a positive that quick. I was dead set in my mind that this was all just one big mistake.

Bryan, on the other hand, was just as convinced that the test was right. So, the next day on the way to school I called Planned Parenthood to set up a time for an official test. I wasn't sure how they did the tests, whether they took blood or not, but there was no way I was going to call my regular pediatrician for a pregnancy test.

I made the appointment at Planned Parenthood for the next Wednesday. Obviously I wasn't in much of a rush to find out. I was in complete denial, still convinced that the positive test result was wrong. I like to call those days between that Sunday and Wednesday when I went to Planned Parenthood my Naïve Phase. These were the days where I stuck my head in the sand and just assumed that there was no way I was pregnant.

CHAPTER 4

Lindsay

THE FINAL
VERDICT IS IN

As you already know, the visit to the clinic didn't go as expected. Who knows how many times that nurse had to walk in to the exam room and deliver bad or unexpected news to other girls. With no emotion at all, she just walked in and said, "The test is positive; you're pregnant. It looks like you're five weeks along. The baby is due August 7th." That was it. My life was drastically falling apart, and this lady was blank faced. My verdict was reduced to bullet points, just bullet points.

- You're pregnant

- You're five weeks along

- The baby is due on August 7th

On the inside, my body just shut down. Time stopped. Confusion, pain, anxiety, and fear were all surging through my body at the same time at 100 miles per hour. I felt like a computer on overload. Everything stopped. My brain was frozen and just as empty and blank as that nurse's face. I found out later from Bryan that while the nurse was giving us the abortion plan, I was in complete shock. All I could focus on was those ugly brown cabinets in that tiny room. I know I must have been out of it because listening to her talk about abortion was definitely something I would have remembered.

My experience is not unique; it's a typical strategy clinics like this use… talking to a girl about abortion while she is still in total shock, before she's even had a chance to grasp her current situation.

She asked us what we wanted to do, and I just stared at her like a little kid in class who was called on by the teacher but hadn't been paying attention. Bryan replied for both of us. "We don't know. We need to talk about it."

Soon after, we slowly made it to the car. Bryan drove us back to the high school because I was too hysterical to drive. I don't know now how I could've been so naïve. I had been having sex with my boyfriend, and people who have sex get pregnant. But my 18-year-old mind couldn't grasp it, much less accept it. Reality had slapped me hard in the face. My naïve phase was definitely over!

A Ray of Hope

Once we got back, the first person I called was my best friend Rachel. She was the only one who knew I might be pregnant and the only one I'd told that I was going to Planned Parenthood that day. Once I told her the news, she was encouraging and talked so positive about it. She reminded me of Jesus and His love for me and that everything would be okay. She gave me hope!

Rachel told me that I could speak to her mom if I needed someone to talk to. I believe that God put Rachel in my life for that moment to bring me hope. God does that. He brings those people along at just the right

The Final Verdict Is In

time to remind us that no matter what the situation is, God is in control. Rachel was my best friend, but during those dark days, she was also my reminder. She was the friend who held up my spirit when I was too weak. Rachel was there to hold my hand to prove to me that I wasn't alone. She held my heart when my situation was too heavy for me. We all need a Rachel in times of trouble and distress.

The enemy has a "divide and conquer" strategy for all of us. Think about it. How many times have you been tempted to close yourself off when struggling in one area or another? We get hit with something and the first thing we do is cocoon ourselves, shutting ourselves off from everyone we know. Mistakenly we believe we're doing the right thing. In reality we're falling right into the enemy's plan for us.

Meanwhile, in our isolation, we begin to listen to the lies that Satan whispers in our ears. Lies like, "Your sin is too terrible. People will never understand. You'll be shunned. People will turn on you and say horrible things about you." You convince yourself that the worst thing you can do is to talk to someone to get your secret off your chest and out in the open. You continue to bury your pain and you suffer alone, which only makes things worse.

But God uses the people in our lives to hand-hold us through these dark times of our soul. God comes to us and comforts us in the form of friends and family who surround us and shine their lights on us. That's why community is so important and isolation is so dangerous. Pulling away by yourself is rarely a good thing. We all need each other and have the responsibility to hold one another closely in love anytime we're hurting.

The Honeymoon Phase

The conversation with Rachel helped me to see the bright side. This pregnancy could actually be a good thing. Over the next several days, I fantasized about how fun this could be to raise a sweet baby and how I would get married to my high school sweetheart and we'd have a perfect little family. We'd move in together and all three of us would be so in love.

I did careful research on our five-week-old fetus and found out that it was the size of a candy sprinkle. I learned that by now it was already growing little nubby arms and legs. I was so excited that I was going to be a mother! I loved this little one already. I even went to the cake aisle at Walmart to look at just how big a sprinkle was. I took a picture of the largest sprinkle I could find to celebrate how big my baby was. During the daytime, my life was great and the thought of having a baby was a dream come true. Sure, maybe it wasn't my dream of being a news anchor, but doesn't every girl dream of having a baby of their own? This dream just came a little earlier than I expected.

But nighttime was a different story. That's when my dream became a nightmare. The dark silence haunted me with reality. Every night I had multiple nightmares about telling my parents. I would only sleep for a couple of hours, then wake up and cry the rest of the night. Whenever I was alone, that's when the fear would set in. I could always convince myself to be happy during the daylight hours, but in the dark of night it was all very clear that I was in trouble.

I don't know what it is about the night, but everything seems magnified. The things you might think about during the day don't worry you half as much as when you think the same thoughts at night. I struggled to fall asleep each night and if I ever woke up in the night, I would have a terrible time trying to go back to sleep.

The next day, Bryan left school in the middle of the day to visit the out-of-state college. He gave me a kiss on the forehead before he took off, and told me that everything would be all right. I tried to put on a brave face, but the truth was, I didn't want him to leave.

Dying Dreams

Before he left, Bryan and I made a plan to tell our parents the Monday night after he came home. But the weekend ended up being so busy for him that I barely got to talk to him at all. I had mixed emotions. I wanted him to be happy and to be able to live his dreams, but at the same time, I wanted him to choose us. It turns out he had the time of his life that weekend at the college. He got to see what his future would look like. Except, of course, that he had a pregnant girlfriend back home.

Sure enough, while he was there, they gave him a college offer. I was trying to be happy for him, but I was confused about where that left us as a couple and the fact that I was pregnant with his baby.

That Friday, I remember experiencing just a little taste of how much my life was going to change. My grandpa ("Buddy") was over at the house, and we were talking about my next steps of going to college. My mom was bragging on me, telling him how I wanted to be a news anchor. I was across the room folding laundry and casually said, "Ehh, I don't know if that's what I want to do anymore."

Mom looked shocked and asked why. I told her that it would be hard to pursue a career like that and still be a mom. Plus, being a news anchor is super competitive. She just kept saying, "Really? Where's this change coming from?" I just kept trying to play if off while I was fighting back tears.

I think that's the first time I felt my dream die. It's the first time I tasted the sacrifice that this was going to take. Little did I know that I was going to get a big spoonful of sacrifice later on. The conversation that day felt like a punch to the gut. The realization that now my life will never be what I thought it would be. Now my goals and my future would be filled with diapers and midnight feedings.

Later that night my parents were getting ready to go to my dad's company Christmas party. I was in my mom's bathroom talking to her as she got ready to go, helping her with her outfit and making small talk. I just kept thinking in my head, this is the last time things will be the same between us. This is the last time things will feel normal in this house. This is the last time my mom will think of me the same way ever again. I just kept saying to myself, "If she only knew. If she only knew." That night I tried to soak up every moment of "normal" I could. I was grasping to stay in that moment where my parents still thought of me as a "good" daughter. I wanted to live in that moment, stay in that place of being the "perfect" family.

I knew the ripple effect of my secret was coming soon; I knew I couldn't keep it hidden much longer. But the revelation of my secret would cause much more than just ripples. News of my pregnancy would be a tsunami of destruction to those I loved the most. That's the problem with our sin-caused storms; they affect more than just us. They crash into the lives of others close to us, people who had no part in our sin, people who had no vote or say in what we did. But now they have to deal with the storm damage just like we do.

CHAPTER 5

Scarlet

UNEXPECTED SATURDAY MORNING

still remember the quiet Saturday morning my whole life was turned upside down. I was sitting in my recliner journaling about my number one priority in life, mothering my three daughters.

Looking back, I can see that over the years I had slowly put my children before everything else in my life. I had allowed them the top spot in my time and my priorities. Certainly our children should be very important, but even the good gifts we receive from God can become idols in our lives if we're not careful. The fact is that anything we put before God in our devotion, time, and adoration is an idol.

When I was a child, I had made a vow to be a better mother to my children than my mother had been to me. That, combined with the fact that I was living in a child-centered culture, worked together to cause my priorities to get jumbled up and out of order.

I was constantly mentally checking and rechecking my precious daughters' needs and wants, like tender plants placed in my care with each one requiring different levels of sunlight, water, and fertilizer. Was the prom dress ironed? Was I home in the afternoon just in case they needed to emotionally dump their heart on me from a long school day? Was their soccer uniform clean and carpool set up?

Besides being a wife and mom, I had been given many opportunities to share with women's groups and enjoyed every minute of mentoring young moms. But lately my ministry had undergone a shift. My new purpose was to help my dad with my mom, who was struggling with severe dementia.

That morning as I journaled, God was reassuring me that even though I felt frustrated with the current circumstances involving my mom, I would soon be entering into a new season, a season of teaching women and being able to share with them all the things that the Lord had been teaching me. As I sat there praying and journaling, I could feel a sense of joy and excitement for what He had planned for my future begin to well up inside my spirit.

My husband Brad came into the room and sprawled out on the carpet. I watched, as he lay on his back, throwing a racquetball up in the air, catching it, and then throwing it up again. I was grateful to have such a wonderful supportive partner in my life.

I sensed God directing my thoughts. He spoke to my heart and pointed out how strange and shocking it would've seemed as a teenager to have a man as part of my world. But now, after years of marriage, Brad had become a familiar part of my everyday life. I had a sense that God was highlighting that observation to me. I felt Him speak to my heart and say that just like Brad is now part of my everyday life, there is something coming that would shock me at first, but that I was to trust Him. It would end up becoming a familiar part of my world and would be a very good thing.

The Bombshell

As our casual Saturday morning together unfolded, Brad made pancakes and Gabrielle, our 8th grader, laid in our bed, covered in our big soft comforter, enjoying the morning off from school. She was flipping through the television channels trying to decide which one to land on and asked as I walked into the room, "Mom, there's a movie on called 'Juno.' Do you know what it's about? Is it good?"

"It's about a girl who gets pregnant in high school," I casually answered. "She's gotta go to school pregnant in front of everyone." Gabrielle paused for a second and said, "Man, that would be a bummer."

I headed out to the kitchen to get started cleaning up the breakfast dishes. With my hands in soapy water, I was still giddy over the prospect of something new coming into our lives. Something really good? I figured it must be future ministry opportunities that the Lord was preparing for me. My view of His plans ended up being quite different from His as is so often the case.

Isaiah 55:8 says, "'For my thoughts are not your thoughts, neither are your ways my ways,' declares the Lord." We all know that God doesn't think like we think, and He doesn't do the things we would do. That may seem obvious, but it's surprising how often we forget the basic truth of that verse. Often, in times of trouble, we can fall into the trap of imagining that His solution to our problem is the same solution that we would come up with.

But He thinks and acts on a much higher plane than we do. His perspective is completely different than ours is. We can only see so much from our limited perspective. God, on the other hand, sees from a much higher, broader perspective. He sees things in our future that we can't see or even imagine. He's able to prepare us for the things that lie ahead, even though we can't see them or even know they're coming.

I was confident that I had heard a wonderful word from God about my future. But He meant something different than I could have comprehended in that moment.

That Saturday morning, Lindsay was still at the breakfast table. She asked us, "So, what do you guys have planned for the day?"

Brad mentioned something about possibly making a run to Lowe's. He started to say more, but was interrupted by a guttural sob that I had never heard from my daughter before. Lindsay wept and moaned at the same time, her body wracked with grief. Her long brown hair covered her face as her entire head hung over from her neck like a rag doll.

Brad and I immediately rushed to her exclaiming, "What's wrong? What's wrong?" Through heaving sobs she finally got out the two words I never expected, two words that would forever change our lives. "I'm pregnant," she sobbed.

It's amazing how quickly things can change. You can be sailing along with no troubles at all and your whole life can turn on a phone call, a text, an email, or a police officer coming to your front door. Rarely are we prepared for these changes when they happen. In my case, I was nowhere near prepared for the change my life was about to take when I heard those two simple words. But words have the power to change our lives all the time.

In the Bible, Gideon's life was changed when he heard, "The Lord is with you, mighty warrior!" (Judges 6:12). Joshua's life was changed when he heard the words, "Moses my servant is dead..." (Joshua 1:2). The disciples' lives were forever changed when Jesus looked at them and said, "Follow me." And let's not forget that the very course of all our destinies was changed when Jesus uttered the words, "It is finished" (John 19:30).

Reality Sinks In

For me in that moment, it was as if time stood still. So many thoughts rushed to my mind I couldn't get them out fast enough. My first response was, "No! Why didn't you tell me that you and Bryan were struggling physically? I could've helped you!" In the midst of my whirling thoughts, one in particular floated up through the chaos. I remembered a conversation I had with my two older daughters only a couple months before. I literally begged them to make good decisions sexually. I had point-blank asked them if they were struggling. Lindsay got frustrated with me and responded arrogantly, "Mom, haven't you seen my relationship with Bryan? I rule the relationship! He will do anything I want, and he knows that I am not having sex until I get married."

I remember ending the conversation with, "Seriously, I'm really worried about what you guys are doing."

I once heard a sermon where the pastor said that it's our fear that opens the door and allows negative things to come into our home. For months this statement haunted me. Now I questioned if the fear of my girls having premarital sex somehow caused this pregnancy. I wondered if somehow I was at fault for not keeping a closer watch on my girls.

Lindsay responded, still through tears, "I knew you'd blame yourself, Mom." With that, I couldn't stand it any longer. I had to get out of the room. I had to move, to do something. I thought if I could go out of the room and reenter, then maybe the last several minutes would have never happened. It was all so surreal. Maybe if I went to another part of the house, then somehow it would rewind the clock and I could come back to a place where my parenting life was neat and tidy and under control—back to a time when we had three daughters who, while not perfect, were staying under the protective wing of the Almighty.

As I rushed from the room, I thought of my daughters. I saw them in my mind as three little girls who had bows for their long hair that perfectly matched the outfits they wore, three little girls whose Momma had poured her entire life into making sure they knew the formula for success. That if they were obedient and did what we told them, then our Christmas card would continue to show a family who could declare just how good and faithful God is, how His ways lead to clean, matching outfits, big smiles, and even a flealess family dog.

Only moments before, my family wasn't perfect, but we were on track. We were lining ourselves up for three weddings to sons-in-law, young men we didn't even know yet but had been praying for since we brought our baby girls home from the hospital. We were on track for big family vacations that included all three girls and their husbands and children, our grandbabies, on the beach together playing in the sand. We were on track for exciting celebratory phone calls to my friends, announcing that I was going to be a grandmother.

But now all those dreams were dashed by those two words. Now there would be a senior year of high school with a pregnant daughter. Now there would be a precious newborn baby born into a world without a stable mother and father, a precious baby who didn't deserve a life of chaos, drama, and upheaval.

I cried out in my mind, *"This wasn't the plan! This wasn't the way things were supposed to work out! Every child deserves to be celebrated and safe, raised by selfless adults. This isn't fair! This baby shouldn't have to be hidden. Pregnancy shouldn't be a shameful thing."*

CHAPTER 6

Scarlet

DAZED AND CONFUSED

The next several hours that day passed in a blur. I remember hearing Gabrielle crying on the couch, "Lindsay, how could you do this? We are the Pepin girls! This doesn't happen to us!" Lindsay sat on the floor of our bedroom leaning up against the armoire in a daze, just staring at the floor.

That evening, Brad and I, along with Gabrielle, drove to a Christmas party at a friend's house, still stunned at the news we'd heard earlier that day. We were quiet as we watched the highway pass beneath our car, each of us lost in our own cloudy thoughts.

The 40-minute ride to the party was often interrupted by our random shell-shocked outbursts. The darkness of the car seemed the perfect place for each of us to process the news in our own way. One of us would quietly say, "I just can't believe it." Ten minutes or so would pass, then another one of us would speak out our thoughts, "I wonder if she will be showing by the time graduation gets here?"

Our questions were rhetorical, none of us expecting them to be answered. We were just unable to keep our thoughts to ourselves. We wanted company;

we wanted to be assured that we weren't alone, that someone else agreed with us. There was a silent sense of betrayal that filled the car. Why does one family member's choice get to shake the entire family?

Of course, this happens all the time. A husband who doesn't believe in divorce, doesn't want a divorce, gets served divorce papers. A wife who believes in the sanctity of marriage and works hard to stay true to her husband, finds out her husband has had an affair with another woman. Parents who believe that substance abuse is wrong and have been diligent to teach that message to their kids, often end up attending classes, learning how to deal with substance abusers. These are sins they never pursued, maybe never even been tempted with, but now have to deal with.

Our sin always bleeds into the lives of others. What we believe will only affect us ends up affecting many, many more. Sometimes when the sin isn't dealt with, it can even affect generations to come. That's the devastation that comes when we don't take sin seriously.

We attended the party that night in a daze. We casually ate Christmas cookies and made small talk around the room, asking about how others were doing. When we were asked about how things were going with us, we demurred, giving polite responses about long lists of Christmas shopping that still needed to be done, or the Branson trip we were planning right after Christmas, or the anticipation of some much needed vacation time away from work and school. While all of these things were true, they weren't what our minds were on that evening.

A Word in Season

That night Brad and I lay side by side in bed. Our room was dark and quiet. Brad's whisper broke the silence. I heard this devoted father declare with a crackling voice and a broken heart, "The formula doesn't work." I reached across and wiped away a tear from his masculine cheek. He continued, "You are told if you raise them right … we even went to the 'Growing Kids God's Way' classes! I gave them each a purity ring to wear. I met every boy at the door who wanted to take out my daughters on dates. I looked them in the eyes and made sure they knew I was a protective and involved dad. With Lindsay, I should've told her she couldn't date Bryan, but I didn't want to control her. I was afraid that if I laid down the law, then she'd rebel."

I was listening intently to his words because his words revealed his heart. Brad was being tormented because he felt responsible. Lindsay was often emotionally volatile during their dating relationship, but Brad could never put his finger on the issue. He'd had a "check" in his gut, in his spirit, that something wasn't right. But he had failed to act. More truthfully, he wasn't sure if he should do something or not.

Yes, he could have forbidden their dating, but we had both believed that Lindsay was telling us the truth—that there was nothing unhealthy or hidden going on.

After tossing and turning for what seemed like hours, Brad finally rolled over and tried to fall asleep, even though the guilt that this mess had happened on his watch had set in.

I was restless too, wishing sleep would come but it never did. What a day it had been, starting with pancakes, sunshine, and optimism, anticipating the promise from God that something new was on the way. I would've never guessed that the day would end with me and Brad trying to grasp the crippling news that our high school daughter was pregnant.

I cried out to God from deep in my spirit, realizing that it was the first time I had turned to Him for help all day. I had spent lots of time that day thinking about me and how Lindsay's news was going to affect my family, but I had neglected to actually turn to God and ask Him what He thought about the situation.

Wouldn't it be nice if it was always our first nature to ask God what He thought before we reacted with emotion? Even those of us who have walked with God for many years can allow the swirling feelings or circumstances of the moment to carry us away and often hours or even days can pass before we remember to seek Him out.

Of course, Jesus knew this tendency of ours. In fact, He speaks directly to this in His "Sermon on the Mount." In Matthew 6:33 He says, "But seek first his kingdom and his righteousness, and all these things will be given to you as well." This is yet another verse about the importance of keeping priorities in line. When we go to God first, the Bible says He will give us the other things we are asking for. When we are careful to get our priorities straight by placing Him first, everything else has a way of falling into line.

I opened my heart … and my ears and asked the Lord, "Please speak to me." Even though I didn't understand their full meaning, I was comforted with His words as I heard His still, small voice say to my heart, "You've been promoted."

The previous year I told God I wanted a life full of adventure and total surrender to Him. Little did I know at the time what that kind of prayer would yield in our lives. "You've been promoted" was good news, exciting news. But it came with an important caveat. Sacrifice would be required. It's an important key of God's Kingdom backed up by scripture. Luke 12:48 says, "From everyone who has been given much, much will be demanded; and from the one who has been entrusted with much, much more will be asked." God does give us great and wonderful gifts, but He expects us to invest those gifts back into the Kingdom and not simply squander them for our own pleasure.

I now know that my "promotion" was all about God leading our family through a journey that would expose my own religious heart, change my husband's understanding of God's grace, and bring Lindsay to a place of total reliance on Him.

God wants to bring growth and life out of what seems, at first, to be tragedy. He is a redeeming God who promises to bring about the best. In fact, that's the story of the Bible … God's redemption of man back to Himself, the whole purpose of Jesus Christ coming to Earth. Of course, that's a perspective often only seen in hindsight. That night, lying in bed, I was overwhelmed just thinking about the long hard road ahead.

Learning to Bite My Tongue

The whole family, except for Lindsay, visited my in-laws' church the next morning. Lindsay, understandably, had asked if she could please stay home and we consented. The drama and emotional upheaval she had experienced the day before would have wiped out most any teenager, but especially one in the beginning stages of her first trimester of pregnancy.

We stood together in our row at church trying to concentrate on the praise and worship, but still reeling from the blow we'd received the day before. Both my daughters were crying, and I had to fight back tears as well. Here we were, surrounded by extended family and friends, trying our best not to let our emotions show. I couldn't help but wonder what they would think if we shared with them exactly why we were crying.

Holding on to a secret can be excruciating and exhausting, but there are times in life when we know that God is asking us to hold our tongue. In the many months that followed, I had to continually rely on His gift of self-control to keep my mouth shut. I know myself, and I'm an external processor. Being able to talk through an issue is critical for me. In this case, I needed to talk about things and express my emotions, but I knew that this was not my story to tell. This was Lindsay's story, and she needed to feel safe in order to walk it out.

Verses like Proverbs 21:23 MSG, "Watch your words and hold your tongue; you'll save yourself a lot of grief," helped me to remember to shut up. And James 3:3-5 states, "When we put bits into the mouths of horses to make them obey us, we can turn the whole animal. Or take ships as an example. Although they are so large and are driven by strong winds, they are steered by a very small rudder wherever the pilot wants to go. Likewise the tongue is a small part of the body, but it makes great boasts. Consider what a great forest is set on fire by a small spark." I had to bite my tongue a lot.

This tongue biting would later become a principal weapon in my self-control arsenal that would be used over and over again as women opened up their hearts and shared their secret prayer requests with me. I can see now that God was developing a spiritual muscle in me that He knew was going to need to be strengthened for the encounters He had planned for my future.

Another benefit to this denial of the desire to blab my emotions had to do with my parenting. As parents, we know from the very beginning that our children are put in our lives to raise and nurture, not to own. Our children truly don't belong to us; they belong to God. Of course, that's something I could've told you on an intellectual level but emotionally, my heart wasn't there. Respecting Lindsay's wishes to not tell a soul was one of the first steps I took in releasing my tentacles of motherly control.

CHAPTER 7

Scarlet

WHAT NOW?
WHAT DO I DO?

It was Monday morning and I had been walking around with the news for a couple days now. I still hadn't fully wrapped my mind around it, but I figured it was time for me to begin to take the right "motherly" steps towards helping my daughter with her pregnancy. I knew all about how to shop for school shoes, how to set up parent/teacher conferences, arrange play dates, and locate the nearest summer library reading program. But navigating through a teenage pregnancy? I definitely had no grid for that.

But there was something in me that made me think I had to fix this situation. I had always been able to fix every scratch, every hurt feeling, and every middle school drama. But how do I fix this? As mothers, we carry our family's baggage. We pick up their troubles because we believe we can fix them. But this time was different; I couldn't carry this baby for Lindsay. This was something that I couldn't solve. Lindsay made a choice, and I was left with the pieces of baggage from every affected and hurt family member.

I am thankful that we have a Heavenly Father who loves us enough to pick up every heavy piece of baggage and pain we have. Not only is He strong enough to handle it, He longs to ease our burdens in this way. It's in His heart to carry our load. Even though I knew this truth in my head, it was quite another thing to be convinced in my heart. It was tough for me to let go and allow the Lord to carry this weight for me without continually trying to handle it myself. Would I be able to trust Him enough to carry my burdens for me? At this point in the story, I wasn't sure.

My first phone call that morning was to an OBGYN. I knew about Lindsay's visit to the clinic, which absolutely shocked me. Why was it that the only place she knew to go was to Planned Parenthood? It highlighted to me the fact that Planned Parenthood had been very successful in becoming a well-known name and resource in the mind of many teenagers. Regardless, I wanted Lindsay to be seen by a doctor as soon as possible.

Once the appointment was made, the next step was to set Lindsay up with some counseling. She and Bryan both needed someone to talk to, someone other than their parents who could offer them some objective guidance about their options. Should they get married? Should Lindsay try to raise the baby on her own? Should she place the baby for adoption?

I shook the questions out of my head and forced myself into "Logic" mode. Who did I know who could help? Who could I call in this situation? I remembered being in a class about ten years before taught by a professional counselor named Chené. She had shared with the class about counseling unwed mothers trying to decide whether to place their babies for adoption or raise them on their own. With a background like that, she certainly would have had years of experience working with families who had dealt with situations like ours.

I quickly dialed her office before I lost my nerve. Even as I dialed, I had no idea what I was going to say. How could I explain something to someone else that I still didn't understand myself? I love how God often gives us only one simple step at a time. Often we don't know how many steps it is going to take to find His answer. Many times the next step to take is not revealed until we take the first step. I had no idea what to do, but when I needed a wise, listening ear, He brought back the memory of this precious woman to me.

When she picked up, I said, "Chené, this is Scarlet Pepin. I'm not sure if you remember me or not, but I took a class you taught almost ten years ago."

"Yes, I remember you, Scarlet. How are you? What can I do for you?"

"I just need some advice. A friend of mine just found out that her teenage daughter is pregnant. She's a senior in high school, and I remembered that you used to counsel girls who'd found themselves in the same scenario."

She quickly responded, "You're right. But I'm no longer counseling young moms who are walking through the process. But I can refer you to a great organization. One place I know of is Crisis Pregnancy Outreach. It's an outreach of a local church. Have you heard of it?"

"Oh, yeah, I know of the church. Brad and I went there as newlyweds." I immediately remembered the pastor and his passion for the pro-life message.

"So the teenager just told her parents?" asked Chené.

When she asked that question I could no longer stifle my emotions just waiting for an excuse to burst through. I did my best to hold back a cry as the words caught in my throat, "It's my daughter, Chené."

"Oh Scarlet, I'm so sorry. I know how much your heart must be breaking."

I did my best to get the words out, "We are just so shocked … we never saw this coming … I mean, it wasn't like she was out partying all the time … this came out of nowhere." I couldn't hold back my tears any longer. I whispered into the phone, "I don't know what to do."

Healing Words

For the next twenty minutes Chené held my heart in her hands as she gently spoke words of encouragement to me over the phone. Through her countless hours of counseling other parents in my situation, she was able to validate the shock and grief I was experiencing. She'd heard it all before.

She was able to explain to me that a big part of the parents' process is not just grieving the situation, but also having to get over the realization that their child was no longer a virgin. For the first time in the last 48 hours, I felt like I could breathe again. Her knowledge and steady voice gave me the ability to finally exhale. The more my mind was able to relax, the more my spirit was comforted. I was reassured by the fact that I was not the first mother to feel this way and that no matter what decisions were made, there would be the light of a beautiful baby at the end of this dark tunnel.

I broached the subject of Lindsay raising the baby on her own. I told her that Lindsay and Bryan had been boyfriend/girlfriend off and on again since the 8th grade. Chené pointed out how difficult it might be for Lindsay to ever break up with Bryan because many of her key adolescent milestones included him. She was so patient to answer all my questions, but it was what she told me about "open adoption" that was priceless.

A Whole New World

Chené had worked with families who had chosen the open adoption route years ago. She had the privilege of meeting many of those adopted as infants years later, and was pleased to learn how they had benefited from growing up in an open adoption. They told her how fortunate they were to have many loved ones through open adoption—loved ones from four sets of families. They shared how meaningful it was to have their birth parents and grandparents attend their school programs, birthdays, and other significant events. They talked about how this "extended family" was around to not only answer any questions about their adoption but to also offer love and support all along the way. Chené was careful to point out that open adoption is not shared parenting but that the adoptive parents make all parenting decisions while the other family members are there to offer support, not advice.

This was a whole new world for me. I was hearing these terms for the very first time. Chené explained the difference between an open adoption and a closed adoption. I learned that a closed adoption is when the biological parents do not want the child to know who they are whereas an open adoption is where both the biological parents and the adoptive parents think it's beneficial for all involved to be a part of the child's life.

I tried to wrap my mind around this new concept. "Doesn't that make the adoptive parents feel threatened or jealous?"

"On the contrary. Parents who are adopting and want an open adoption see the benefits of the child being loved by all those around them. The child knows from the beginning that they were placed for adoption because their birth mother and birth father loved them so much that they wanted the child to have a better life than what the birth parents could offer."

Examples from Scripture

I leaned into the conversation, hanging on every word. Chené explained that open adoption was a concept that ran throughout the Bible. She told me the story of Moses from Exodus 2 and how his Hebrew birth mother put him in a basket, and then placed the basket in among the reeds along the bank of the Nile River. Moses' adopted mother, the Pharaoh's daughter, took him out of the Nile and raised him in the palace. But Moses' birth mother was able to continue to nurse him all the way through his infancy.

Chené continued to explain, "In Acts 7:20-22 it tells us that Moses was educated in the wisdom of the Egyptians." She said, "Isn't it interesting how God, in all His sovereignty, knew that later in life Moses was going to return to Egypt as the deliverer of the Hebrew people?" Moses developed skills in Pharaoh's court that he would need later in life to fulfill his mission as a deliverer.

Moses' adoption was part of his destiny and ultimately part of the sovereignty of God's plan. Moses wasn't going to be able to get all he needed to fulfill his purpose from his biological home; it was going to take the combining of the two families. His first family gave him his raw DNA, his Hebrew roots, while his second family gave him his training in leadership."

I was amazed. I'd never before thought of the story of Moses as a story of adoption. But Chené wasn't finished. She told me about another example of open adoption from the Bible. It's the story of Hannah and her son Samuel found in 1 Samuel 1. Hannah places her son in the care of the priest Eli to be raised by him in the temple after she had weaned him.

In 1 Samuel 2:19 it tells us that every year Hannah would bring Samuel a robe when she visited the temple. Hannah always knew exactly where her son Samuel was, and their relationship continued when she visited the temple every year.

This was a whole different perspective for me, to see that adoption is a good thing, not bad. Chené told me that she believed that there can be a way to adopt children where everyone understands their role and where everybody is committed to helping this precious child fulfill their destiny and purpose. As she spoke, a deep peace filled my soul; and I was beyond grateful that God had led me to this wise woman. She had more examples and shared the beautiful outcomes of each.

She told me about how Mordecai raised his niece Esther after she was orphaned; and when it was time for her to go before the king to save her people, she was equipped and ready because Mordecai had coached her. It was Mordecai, the "adopted father" whom God designated to prepare Esther for her prophetic destiny.

"If you think about it," she continued, "Jesus is another example of open adoption. His true birth father wasn't Joseph; it was God the Father Himself. The Father 'gave up' His Son to Joseph and Mary who became the adoptive parents. Of course, Mary also gave birth to Him.

Jesus knew exactly why He was on this Earth. He also knew His life's plan had to go through Jerusalem and on through Calvary. Jesus knew He had to leave His Father and be adopted by His earthly parents, Mary and Joseph, in order to fulfill His destiny.

Chené showed me that in all four examples, the individuals adopted had a divine prophetic purpose, but had to leave their original birth family and go into a different home in order to achieve it. Certainly there were difficulties that none of these families would have chosen for themselves. But desperate situations require desperate measures. And adoption is often a desperate measure brought about by a desperate situation. But, as Chené explained, "…in all things, God works for the good of those who love him, who have been called according to his purpose" (Romans 8:28).

She shared with me about some of the services that Crisis Pregnancy Outreach (CPO) offered young mothers who didn't choose adoption but rather chose to raise their babies. She also told me about the counseling and health services available and even about the valuable support from other teenagers who were choosing to parent their babies. I had no idea which path Lindsay would choose, but I knew that Crisis Pregnancy Outreach was the organization that would be able to give her all the help she was going to need.

My next call was to CPO and, by God-ordained destiny, the lady who answered the phone was a dear friend of mine. Like getting a huge hug from the other end of the phone line, Kelly listened to my heart and shared her own story of adopting several children.

I'm so grateful that God has not put us on this planet to walk alone. With Lindsay's permission, I had now been able to connect with two women who played a vital role in assuring me that our story would be one of victory and joy-filled destiny. Just like a partially completed painting, I could already see the beginning of God's handiwork and heart behind our story. It was only a rough sketch in my mind at this point, but I had the confidence that with each new brush stroke a new masterpiece would reveal itself.

What a redeeming God we have! He loves taking our mistakes and struggles and shaping them into something that not only brings healing to us, but also has real value to teach and encourage others … if we're just willing to stay open to His process.

CHAPTER 8

Scarlet

ADOPTION?

'd never really considered the idea of adoption before. Of course, I'd never really considered the idea of my teenage daughter becoming pregnant before either. But now that the pregnancy was a reality, I had to consider lots of things I hadn't considered before. In those first few days I was opposed to the idea of adoption, but at the same time, I couldn't see a way for Lindsay to raise the baby on her own. She was at the stage in life where she was very self-centered, believing that the world revolved around her and what she wanted.

So if I wasn't comfortable yet with adoption, and if Lindsay wasn't ready to raise the child, what was left? Thoughts of Brad and me raising the baby would float up in my mind from time to time. The thoughts would swirl and swirl in a confusing tangle. Every time I saw a way through it, I was met with another issue I couldn't resolve. Just about the time I thought I might be gaining some level of clarity about the situation, the fog would roll back in, and I found myself confused all over again.

Of course, before my daughter was pregnant, I had all the answers. I had the perfect response for what someone else should do if they should find themselves in a situation like ours. But now that this was my reality, I had no idea how to move forward. Even today, as I share this story with others, many mothers feel like they know exactly what they would do if they were in our shoes. But the truth is, unless you've ever actually been there, you really don't have a clue. With multiple parties involved, there are multiple voices and opinions. I was learning that theory and reality are two very different things.

With the advantage of hindsight, I can see how God taught me throughout every single stage of my "promotion." I realize that I'm a much different person now than I was then. This chapter of my life has changed me. Today I'm not so quick to "weigh in" on other people's decisions. Before the pregnancy I would have been tempted to decide what I thought another family should do with their children or in their parenting. I may not have ever verbally shared my judgmental opinion, but in my mind I gave myself permission to try their situation on and issue an inner verdict on what I would do if I were in their place. I now know that unless I am in the middle of the story, it is not my place to cast my vote one way or the other.

As I hear mothers share their tragic stories of losing a child or going through a horrific accident, or as I sit across from a mother whose child is in prison, I think, *"Who am I to speak into their situation?"* But because of my experience, I can now listen without judgment and without the arrogance that assumes I could possibly understand what they are going through. No more advice from this Momma, just a listening ear and a finger pointing to the Hero in every story, the only One who can heal and bring peace ... our Jesus.

Jesus is the answer in every situation. He is the One who gives guidance, and the Holy Spirit gives comfort. Whatever life throws at us, He guarantees that He will walk with us through the storm. The wonderful news is that He not only walks with us, but He redeems circumstances even though we can't imagine how He will do it. Through our broken-ness, bewilderment, and pain, He makes all things new.

I love the story of Ruth from the Bible. Ruth was a woman who had lost her husband, and the only family she had left was her mother-in-law Naomi. Naomi urged Ruth to return to her own home and relatives, but Ruth was determined to stay with Naomi. She told her mother-in-law, "Don't urge me to leave you or to turn back from you. Where you go I will go, and where you stay I will stay. Your people will be my people and your God my God" (Ruth 1:16).

What a strong statement of faith! Ruth had endured the terrible loss of her husband, but she trusted in the Lord. Ultimately, Ruth married a man named Boaz who redeemed her loss. So important was their union that they are ancestors of David … and Jesus. Does God redeem seem-ingly hopeless situations? Absolutely!

But at this point in the story, I wasn't feeling full of faith in God; far from it. I was completely blindsided by this life change that had been thrust upon me. But the good news is that now I have a whole new perspective. I can actually say with confidence that I know I was specifically chosen to play a very important role. I was a part of the family chosen to help launch this child into their destiny and chosen to share this story of God's faith-fulness to guide and bless us even when we don't see how.

Lindsay—Going to Counseling

Bryan and I went to counseling that following week through Crisis Pregnancy Outreach. In the session, I just sat there in a daze. I couldn't believe this was happening to me. The counselor asked me probing ques-tions, but I deflected and answered her as quietly and as quickly as possible. I had no concept that she was trying her best to help.

The following Tuesday Bryan and I went to a support group meeting, also through CPO. We chose to attend the adoption group because it was the subject we knew the least about. I was nervous and so anxious to attend the meeting that I couldn't eat at all that day, which is odd for a pregnant girl!

When we got to the meeting, we listened to stories of girls further along than I was and also from girls who had already placed their babies for adoption. All their stories were so different from mine. They had one key ingredient that mine didn't have. Their stories had hope.

I knew that their hope was coming from the fact that they had fully accepted their situation. But they did more than just accept their situation; they'd surrendered their circumstances to God, "surrender" being the key word. "Surrender" means letting go, yielding, giving up, and accepting the inevitable. These people had been able to find their peace because they'd yielded themselves to the process of getting better. They'd found peace through their pain, a peace that came from reaching out and getting help. They had found a peace that passes all understanding (Philippians 4:7).

Although I knew in my mind that going to the support group was best for me, I couldn't help feeling in my heart that I just didn't belong in that group. These people were happy and had hope and a plan. I, on the other hand, was still just trying to get used to the idea that I was even pregnant, let alone trying to make a decision about adoption.

The Worst Christmas Ever

"'Tis the season to be jolly" is what most people say around December 25th. For most people this is a joyous time to celebrate family, togetherness, and Jesus' birth. But there are always a few unfortunate souls who would rather hide from all the joy and laughter because they know they can't possibly feel the holiday spirit. In the words of the Grinch, their heart feels "two sizes too small." This year was the year that will forever be known as "The Worst Christmas Ever."

Like many families, ours had classic Christmas traditions. Every Christmas we enjoyed each other's company, the laughter, the stories, and of course, the gifts. But this year was different. There was another baby in the picture now besides Jesus. There was a dark cloud of sadness hanging in every room.

On this particular Christmas Day, after only a few hours of trying to fake my way through a happy holiday, I just couldn't take it anymore. I had to escape. My head was fuzzy with conflicting emotions. I mean … it was Christmas and I was supposed to be happy, right? But I was also pregnant, which was Issue #1. And I didn't have a clue what to do or how to deal with it, which was Issue #2. My sin had alienated me from my own family … the people I was supposed to feel the closest to, especially at Christmas. But now it was just so awkward. It was exhausting trying to keep up the appearance that everything was normal.

This is what I hated worst of all: I had damaged the relationships I had with my parents and with my sisters. We had always been so close, sharing so much. Now my sin was like the Grand Canyon that stretched out between us, dividing us, keeping us apart. I couldn't figure out a bridge back to them, and that was devastating to me.

I went up to my room to be alone, and it wasn't long before I heard my mom's tentative knock on my door. She had come up to check on me. I told her that I couldn't take the tension any longer and had to come upstairs for some relief. Through many tears, I told her that I was sorry but I didn't know what to do to repair things with her and my dad.

It wasn't long before my dad heard the crying, and he came into my room to see what was going on. Once he heard the conversation, he became upset. It was clear that I had hurt him … badly. He told me that in his mind, the only way to repair things was for me to leave Bryan, once and for all. To him, it was a simple choice between Bryan and my family, and I was choosing Bryan. He shouted that I was choosing this boy over my own father who had raised me and loved me more than anything in the whole world. He finished by telling me that he couldn't be my spiritual covering anymore if I continued to insist on choosing Bryan.

Here I was, at the age of 18, being told that I needed to make a choice between my parents on the one hand and my boyfriend on the other. He didn't use those exact words, but I felt the pressure of having to choose nonetheless. The problem for me was that keeping the baby and keeping Bryan were one and the same thing to me. But that's not the way my dad saw it.

After what had seemed like hours of this kind of conversation, I realized that I had become a stranger in my own home. In my current state of mind, I no longer even felt like Lindsay Pepin. As an empty threat, I told my parents that I would just move into Rachel's house. From my previous conversations with her, I knew her parents wouldn't mind if I moved in; they even had a spare bedroom I could use.

I was totally unprepared for the words that flew out of my dad's mouth. He shouted, "Go, then! Just go!" That was it. I knew then that I had officially lost my family. I was all alone. That feeling was interrupted by the sound of my mom's sobbing. She told me that she couldn't lose me, that I better call her every day, and that she didn't want Rachel's mom to take me to the doctor. She wanted to be the one to go with me.

I could see the pain etched across my mother's face. This perfect little egg that she had held in her hands for so long was cracking. My father, on the other hand, was silent. He was unable to understand why I would continually choose Bryan over his protective covering and care. There was no doubt, my dad wanted Bryan out of the picture.

Once we took a hard look at the choice of me moving out, it was clear to all three of us that we needed to find another solution quickly. We weren't the type of family that has a child move away from home while still in high school.

Eventually, through many tears, I told my dad that I loved him and that I was sorry. What I had done with Bryan had nothing to do with him. I was not trying to choose Bryan over him, but I loved Bryan. The problem was that I loved my dad *and* I loved Bryan. We talked and cried for what seemed to be hours, and finally wore ourselves out. The countless emotions had completely drained each of us … again. We ended the night in the living room with popcorn, a movie, and very puffy eyes.

The Trip to Branson

For most people Christmas ends after December 25th, but when you have a father with nine siblings, you tend to celebrate Christmas at different times of the year when everyone can get together. This was the year that we were scheduled to celebrate Christmas a few days after Christmas Day in Branson, Missouri. If the tension and chaos were not suffocating enough for our family of five in our own home, we got the added joy of all sharing a single bedroom for the next three days. Not only was our family sharing just one bedroom, but we were also sharing a large house with about 32 other family members; 32 other people who had no idea that we were fighting the biggest battle of our lives. Of course, by this time, we'd all become pros at faking our true feelings and wearing our "happy masks."

I knew it wasn't time yet to share my situation with the extended family. I wanted to wait until I got further along in my heart and mind. I wanted to wait for the rest of my immediate family to at least get used to the idea of my pregnancy before I considered sharing the news with everyone else. I was paranoid that once I opened my mouth about the pregnancy that the news would somehow reach my high school. Keeping it from my extended family was hard, but I just wasn't ready to expose myself yet. I needed some things in my life to stay as normal as possible for now.

During our stay in Branson, the women would talk and, of course when women talk, they bring up all their wonderful pregnancy stories, birthing stories, and their weird cravings. They even went around the room and guessed who was going to have the next baby in the family. Of course, it's safe to say that they ALL got it wrong! I couldn't believe it, but they also brought up adoption. I'm sure my face was bright red, but nobody noticed.

Finally, the trip came to an end when our family decided to leave a day early. I think the faking and troubled hearts were wearing thin on all of us. We then endured a quiet four-hour car ride home back to Tulsa.

The Trip to the Doctor

The holidays had settled, and it was time for me to go to my first doctor's appointment. Bryan's mom gave us the name of a female doctor, who oddly enough had both a biological baby and an adopted child. I was relieved, thinking that there was a chance she might understand our situation and the options that we had to consider better than a male doctor. I was hoping I wouldn't be judged.

As soon as my mom and I arrived, they ushered us in for my first ultrasound. We could instantly see the little baby; it looked like a thumb with legs. We could hear the whooshing of the heart and were suddenly overwhelmed with joy. There really was something living inside of me. That ultrasound showed me that there was life with a beating and living heart.

I also received the first photo of my baby. They told me that I was about three months along, a week less than I originally thought. When we were finished in the ultrasound room, we went up to see the doctor. To my relief, the doctor and her nurse were extremely nice and very understanding. I did not feel judged at all, which was great. For the first time, I felt just like a regular pregnant person instead of a dirty teenager. They said that the baby was looking healthy and strong. From there, we went to go get my blood taken just to make sure I didn't have any health concerns that might hinder the baby's growth. At the end of it all, everything was just fine and on schedule, but I was exhausted! It was an extremely emotional day for me. Luckily this time, most of those emotions were happy ones.

The Pain of a Broken Heart

By now, I had experienced many of the big events and firsts of pregnancy. The dust was finally starting to settle around me, but there was nothing settled in my head or my heart. This had become my constant battle, just making it through each day. The days were miserable as I counted down to my due date. I kept thinking, *"IF I can just make it to tomorrow...."* That was my daily goal; just make it to the next day. I couldn't think much further than that. You never think that you might not physically be able to make it to the next day until you go through a trauma like I was going through. The pain, confusion, and stress were overwhelming to the point that it was hard for me to breathe.

When I think about it now, I believe the pain came from the loss of my dreams, the tension in my family, and the heavy decision that SOMEONE ELSE'S life was now fully dependent on me. I was going to have to make a decision that was going to affect and alter someone's full life. The pain was unbearable, but I just had to make it to the next day ... I just had to make it.

Looking back, I regret not being able to see that God had been with me that whole time. There wasn't a single moment that He left my side. It's like I was a little girl, thinking I was walking through a dark cave, terrified that I was all alone, only to discover later that my Heavenly Father had been there beside me the whole time.

Our lives are filled with fits and starts, always moving up or moving down. But through our high highs and low lows, God is always there. He's right by our side. God is faithful … He stays faithful, no matter what. He's faithful to stay with us even when we think we've pushed Him so far away that we can no longer feel His touch and presence in our lives. But He never leaves our side. He is always there, reaching out for our broken hearts. Reaching out to meet us right where we are, ready to hold our hand through it all.

CHAPTER 9

Scarlet

BRAD OPENS UP

thought I was finally coming to grips with how I felt about Lindsay's pregnancy. But the one person I wasn't sure about was the person I knew better than anyone else in this world … Brad. I knew things were stirring in his heart, but I wasn't sure exactly what those deep waters held until we had a conversation one night before going to bed.

He quietly said, "I had lunch with John today. He told me about how Samantha is dating now." John and his wife Veronica were our family friends who were also in the midst of raising three daughters. Their daughters were almost the exact same ages as our girls.

As Brad started to share with me, his deep hurt and confusion tumbled out all at once. "He talked all about how Samantha's date came in and how he looked him straight in the eye and how he made sure the guy knew in no uncertain terms that a strong dad was in the home. He even joked about wanting to have his shotgun visible.

"It was so hard for me to play along. The whole time I'm thinking, *'Yep, I did the same thing, I was there when my girls' dates came to the door. I was the tough dad protecting my daughters.'* I'm sitting there thinking, *'What's he*

59

going to think when he finds out?' I just don't get it, Scarlet. Why me? What did I do wrong? How did we end up here? I went to all of her events, I cheered her on, poured countless hours into loving, mentoring, encouraging, and training. I wasn't some kind of absentee dad!

"It's just so frustrating. Of course I forgive her. We've all messed up before. Mistakes happen to all of us. I don't care about any of that. I just want to scoop up my baby and take care of her. But I just can't understand why she's clinging so hard to Bryan. I want him out of the picture. You don't realize how much dads take pride in protecting their daughters. It's our JOB—we are the protectors! How did this happen on my watch? It pisses me off! Where did I go wrong?"

I didn't know what to say so I opted to keep my mouth closed. How was I supposed to console this father's heart? What could I tell him that would bring any comfort at all? I had never been a father. I knew he was just venting ... not looking for a response. Here was a man who loved his little girl, but his heart was breaking.

I thought of how many times I had hurt my Heavenly Father's heart by choosing to go down a path He hadn't chosen for me. The Bible says we have ALL sinned and fallen short (Romans 3:23). All of us expend so much energy trying to put forward this perfect persona when all the while we're anything but perfect. None of us. We've all done things we're not proud of. We've acted in ways we wish we could take back. But just like Brad had already forgiven Lindsay, God is quick to always forgive us whenever we confess our sins (1 John 1:9).

Ironically, confessing our sins, instead of hiding them, takes the sting out of them, and more importantly, neutralizes their power over us. As long as we tamp them down and try to pretend we've never done anything wrong, those sins loom larger than life. They simmer just beneath the surface always threatening to go public. In that way, they hold power over us.

But when we confess those sins, admit we've fallen short, admit we're not perfect, and recognize that we've sinned against God, He is always faithful to forgive us. And more than that, He forgets our sins too. It's as if they never happened.

There were many times during the pregnancy that Brad and I would share deep emotional moments together. There were very few people who knew our secret, and we were the only two people on the entire planet who had parented Lindsay all these years.

Brad and I were a team and, as tough as those times were, I'd never felt closer to him than I did during those difficult nine months. No one loved Lindsay more than we did, and no one felt more blindsided by her revelation. There was a strange but powerful feeling of "us" between Brad and I that I had never experienced before. We had co-labored and co-loved our Lindsay Joy, and now our baby was pregnant. It is interesting to me how some very good things can manage to spring up in the middle of a storm.

We've all seen news footage of wildfires burning out of control. There's no doubt that forest fires cause untold damage and have the power to bring terrible destruction. But forest fires also have the power to stimulate new growth. When older trees burn down, it opens the forest canopy, allowing sunlight, which had been blocked before, to reach all the way to the forest floor, stimulating new growth.

But that's not all. The heat from the fire actually causes some pinecones to open up, releasing their seeds and bringing a whole new crop of trees to the forest. It's amazing how something so terrible, so destructive, can actually stimulate new growth.

The same is often true in our lives. We love it when everything is going along great. But the truth is, real growth, real change, occurs during trials. There's an old saying, "Necessity is the mother of invention." It's human nature that we rarely look for new ideas until the old ideas no longer work.

We love the view from the top of the mountain, but nothing grows up in the rarified air of the summit. The lush growth is all in the valley below. It's the difficult times of life that cause us to exercise new spiritual muscles. Tough times create strong faith. Sure, Lindsay's unplanned pregnancy had the potential to burn our family to the ground, to put a wedge between Brad and me. But God was faithful to redeem the pain and confusion with which we were dealing. And the heat from that fire actually stimulated new growth in our marriage. We are not the same couple we were before the fire. The difficulties we encountered made us a much stronger couple, and that's made us a much stronger family.

God uses every circumstance to bring good to those who love Him and are called according to His purpose (Romans 8:28). As Christians we can confidently stand on this promise. But this can be a tough truth for our logical minds to accept. We want answers! We ask, "Why did this happen, God? How in the world are You going to bring good out of this?"

We all go through struggles. And even though our struggles may look different, they all reveal a single, common truth. God will never leave our side. He will walk with us all the way through our struggle; and if we lean into Him, He will unfold a blessing we can't imagine.

When the storm finally subsides, we will see again and again how faithful our Heavenly Father has been. When the raging wildfire finally blows itself out, we have confidence that new growth will return to the forest.

In the months that followed, I would discover new facets of God's faithfulness that I had never known before. One of my favorite discoveries was realizing that my marriage was a safe place of refuge for me.

Lindsay—Changes at School

Unlike most expecting mothers, I still had high school to deal with. My senior year I decided to earn college credits by taking a few classes at the local community college. This allowed me to stay home three days a week until third period. The two other days, I was able to lose myself in the crowd at the local community college. No one at the college knew me and couldn't have cared less about whether I was pregnant or not. For all they knew, I was just a weepy high schooler and I liked it that way. Being invisible was great. It was easy and I was good at it. Plus I didn't have to stand around in the halls making small talk all the time.

After my college class, I would leave for my high school. As I drove from one place to the other, it always felt like an out-of-body experience to me, like I was watching someone else drive my car. I never had to think about how to get there, so I could drive my old red Mazda on autopilot. On the drive to the high school, I would mentally prepare myself for the private war I knew I would be fighting for the rest of the day. Because no one at school knew yet, I had to gear myself up for my grand performance every single day.

My favorite break of the day was my once-a-class period bathroom break … I was usually desperate thanks to the baby pushing on my bladder. While everyone was still in class, I would be alone in the bathroom looking at myself in the mirror. In the past, that mirror reflected a girl who loved life, someone confident, sure of herself, and sure of where she was going in life. But these days the girl looking back at me was shaking her head with sad, empty eyes, eyes that revealed the denial and confusion felt inside. In that mirror I saw a girl who was lost and unsure of herself, confused about what was happening, and not knowing what was going to happen. As I would leave the bathroom, I had to hide the hurt, pain, and confusion, pretending to be upbeat and happy.

CHAPTER 10

Lindsay

THE HARDEST CHOICE

There was a trade-off of being at school. Although school was filled with its struggles and battles, at least I didn't have to be an adult there. At school I wasn't required to discuss how I felt or have to talk about making major life decisions. Most importantly, I knew that at school I could talk about something other than being pregnant. When I was home I didn't have to deal with keeping secrets, but everyone at home was still digesting the news of a baby growing inside me. My mom constantly wanted to talk, and my pregnancy was her favorite topic. She's always had to discuss things in order to process them.

But I'm different. I usually avoid talking about things; and with my pregnancy situation, I preferred the numb feeling of denial. Denial was safe. When I wasn't in denial, I would think, *"I CANNOT TAKE THIS ANOTHER MINUTE! I need to just die and the pain will stop."*

There was even one day, my darkest day, when I realized, *"I can just make this baby disappear."* It was the first time in my life that I could understand how someone could abort their baby. The pain is so deep and all consuming that you fool yourself into believing that you can just make it all disappear. Now that is true denial. A baby is alive whether inside the womb or out. The truth was, I was already a mother. I was already a caretaker, even though the baby hadn't been born yet.

Though the pain was all consuming, it could not outweigh the love I had for this baby. The pain couldn't outweigh the hope and the destiny I knew this baby possessed. There was no way that my pain justified a loss of life, not the baby's nor mine. I knew an abortion would not fix the pain. In fact, an abortion would only cause more pain. I came to realize that the pain I was feeling was out of love. The battle in my mind was over making the right decision for MY baby. I loved that baby, and from the moment its little heart started to beat inside of me, we began to bond. I knew there was life inside me, and I was reminded of that fact every day as I sat at my desk at school and felt that tiny, joyful kick.

I was so blessed to have people in my life who supported me during this painful journey. People who made sure I knew that my baby and I were treasured, that we had value. It's so important to realize that everyone has value, no matter what. There's not a mistake we can make or a pain we can bear that will lessen our value. All our lives are precious. The lives of babies, lives of children, lives of adults, they all have purpose. Everyone has been born for a purpose; they've been loved since the day they were conceived by their Creator.

Scarlet—Abortion Stops a Beating Heart

As newlyweds Brad and I participated in a pro-life event at our church. The church had made professionally printed signs that said, "Abortion Stops a Beating Heart." Brad and I joined our fellow church members standing along one of the busiest streets in Tulsa holding up these signs.

One of our outspoken friends said, "When people drive by, we need to give the 'thumbs-up' sign, asking them nonverbally if they agree or disagree. That way we're more engaging, asking them how they feel about the issue." He was right. When we just held the cardboard signs, people would sometimes honk or nod, but when we put our thumbs up, the drivers would look and respond by either giving us the thumbs up or the thumbs down. Some refused to give their opinion and would just scowl or avoid making eye contact altogether.

The people in the cars were being confronted with a difficult question in the middle of their private world inside the bubble of their car, "Does abortion stop a beating heart?" A lot of Americans really don't want to face that reality. We want to be left alone to drive our cars, get lost in our music, and drink our coffee. That is, until the possibility of abortion affects our home, or our daughter, or our future plans.

I was so proud of Lindsay when, a whole year before becoming pregnant, she told me about a conversation she'd had with one of her teachers at her public high school. Somehow they got on the topic of abortion, and this teacher said that if he found out through a medical test that one of his unborn children had issues, he and his wife would abort the baby. Lindsay was bold enough to speak out and tell him that there was no way she could ever kill an unborn child.

Now here it was, one year later, and she was pregnant. She had to summon the courage not only to take a stand in the classroom, but to stick to her convictions in her own situation. Ultimately, my daughter bravely decided to walk out her belief in front of our family, our church, and all of her peers.

Why Didn't I See This Coming?

There were many days that my mind wandered, trying to determine my next step. What was my role supposed to be? I would buy prenatal vitamins for Lindsay and would go through my daily duties, but my mind never seemed to stop thinking about how this was all going to work out. I cried out to God, "I don't know what I'm supposed to do, I feel so disoriented."

I felt a little like Noah hearing from God and building a huge ark for a flood that hadn't even happened yet. Noah wasn't a shipbuilder, probably not even a carpenter, and yet the Lord had asked him to build an ark though there wasn't an ocean in sight. I'm sure there were days when he questioned himself, just like I did. "What's going on? What in the world am I doing?"

I felt Him speak to my heart, "That's how all people feel when they are new on the job. They don't know where the stapler is or how to use the copier. I told you that you have been promoted to this new place. Just take one step at a time."

Promotion? I thought promotion would feel better than this!

I'd never thought about it before, but when you're promoted you may get more pay or a bigger office but more times than not, you're also confronted with new challenges, new battles, and new things to learn. In my case, my "promotion" had completely thrown me off. Nothing in my past had prepared me for what I was going through with my daughter's pregnancy. Every day, every step seemed to hold layers and layers of uncertainty.

There were days that I wrestled with guilt. Why wouldn't God reveal to me what was going on with Lindsay? Why would God show me prophetic things about other situations and talk to me about His inner thoughts but not give me a head's-up that my daughter had been lying to me all along?

He brought me back to a dream I had had a few weeks before Lindsay had told us about the baby. In my dream I saw a picture of a little toddler girl. I didn't know who she was because I couldn't see her face, but she was standing next to a grill, the kind you cook burgers on outside on the patio. She was wearing a puffy winter coat. I remember thinking at the time, *"She's too small to be standing so close to the grill!"* I woke up, not in panic but in complete peace and no fear.

Now God was reminding me of that dream, but this time with an interpretation of what the dream meant. I realized that the little girl in the dream was "out of season." You don't wear a winter coat at a summer barbeque.

Now I realized that the little girl in the dream was Lindsay. She was "out of season," having sex outside of marriage. God could have shown me her face in the dream but He didn't. I remembered that I was at total peace when I woke up.

God didn't give me all the details because Lindsay, like all of us, has her own free will. God has given us all the freedom to choose, and it is not up to me as the parent to control Lindsay's every decision.

Free will is such an interesting but critical ingredient in our relationship with God as well as in the love relationships we have with others. Think about it. God could've created us with our love for Him built in … we'd just naturally love Him. But is that real love? Is it real love when you have no choice to do otherwise? No.

The same is true in our relationships. I choose to love Brad as my husband. He doesn't make me love him. I choose to love him, and that's what makes my love precious to him.

In the same way, God wants us to want to choose Him. He doesn't want us to love Him just because we have no choice in the matter. That's why free will is so important. Lindsay had to make her own choices. They weren't mine to make.

I felt a new assurance that God was not surprised that Lindsay was sleeping with her boyfriend. In one of those little mental leaps your brain makes, I realized that the night I had had that dream was during the same month that Lindsay and Bryan were sleeping together.

God was showing me that He was God, and He had given Lindsay the freedom to make her own choices. My role was to be Lindsay's mom, and I had to quit blaming myself for not knowing everything that was going on in my child's life.

A Friend to Share My Secret

Keeping a secret is hard! And for an external processor like me, it's doubly difficult. The only people I could talk to were my family, and most of the time they had no desire to talk through these things with me. It took a while, but I finally convinced Lindsay that, for my own mental health, I had to be able to share her secret with at least one friend.

I chose one of my best friends, Dawn, to reveal our secret to. I found a great deal of comfort in finally being able talk with someone about what I was going through. She was very understanding and emotionally held my hand throughout our entire journey. Dawn became the one who helped carry my heart, just like Rachel did for Lindsay. Mental isolation will drive us to loneliness; everyone needs a safe person with whom to be honest and vulnerable.

I hit Dawn with all my random thoughts over the phone one day. "Do you think I should pull Lindsay out of school? I mean, this may be just too much for her. I guess it will depend on when she starts showing. I'll homeschool her if I have to so she can graduate on time."

It was a relief to be able to talk off the top of my head and process all my questions without having to tiptoe around the minefield of emotions that now filled my home. Like a teapot arriving at the boiling point, this momma had to whistle! The comfort of a loving friend's ear was a gift straight from heaven for me.

Project Left Out in the Rain

"How's it going?" Dawn asked one day during one of our phone calls. "I've been crying a lot recently. I think I'm grieving Lindsay's lost future. Like what her future could have been."

"Can you tell me more about that?" she gently asked, more like a wise counselor than a close friend.

"Lindsay was in my care, and I didn't protect her. The only way I can explain it is that it's like when she was born I was given a project. Almost like a blank page from a scrapbook. This was "the page of Lindsay." I decorated it detail by detail, year by year. Picking out her clothes, rocking her as a newborn, telling her Bible stories, and nurturing her any way I could."

I choked back the tears as I tried to explain. "And then someone left my beautiful page outside in the rain all night. The marker I used to decorate my page is now running and smeared, and it's left me grieving and heartbroken."

Dawn whispered, "What a clear description." I knew that her mother's heart had understood exactly how I felt. It was such a blessing to have Dawn to talk to about this. Talking with her had helped me finally put words to what I was feeling.

Every mother, at some point in her child's life, has to realize that her children are in her care for only a short time, and she doesn't get to possess them. To really love a child is to prepare them for the future they will choose for themselves when they leave your care. Sure, I had dreams and aspirations for my little girl. I had expectations of what I hoped she'd be when she grew up. But ultimately, the path was going to have to be her path, her choice.

I wasn't really aware of this fact until I began the process of slowly releasing, just a little bit at a time, my maternal grip from my expectations of what Lindsay's life was supposed to have been. It was one of the hardest things I'd ever done, but little did I know I was only in the beginning stages of letting her go. I still had a long road ahead.

CHAPTER 11

Lindsay

CHOICES

As the months went by, there were decisions that had to be made; but whether Bryan and I were ready to make them or not was another matter. We were constantly weighing out all the options and overthinking every scenario. Bryan was going to college. I, on the other hand, had no idea what I wanted to do. I had no shortage of input. I listened carefully to what others in my CPO support group were saying, and of course, there were the daily conversations with my mom.

I indulged myself in the possibility that I could actually be the mom I always wanted to be. I pictured the smiling little baby looking up at me with a no-crust sandwich firmly in a chubby little hand while sitting in a designer high chair in a beautiful large kitchen. I would be the suburban mom who had it all. Of course, I had to constantly remind myself that was just a wild dream. The reality was that I was an 18 year old with no job and no husband. But I loved my baby, and it was hard for me to let go of the idea of having a child of my very own.

But this was no time for dreaming. I had to get logical. In my mind, everything boiled down to four options:

A.   I keep the baby and understand that Bryan would see the child whenever he would be in town. I would have to find some type of job where the baby could accompany me to work. I'd have to figure out some kind of living situation between my parents' home and moving out on my own. I would do the "single mom" thing, and try to better my life and grow up while at the same time trying to support a child. Then, when Bryan graduated from college, we'd work out some kind of arrangement where he would get the baby every other weekend. I hoped that Bryan would be able to provide child support. Along with Option A came some fears. Bryan's parents might want the baby every other weekend while he is in college. They might even try to get full custody. Bryan could graduate and marry someone wonderful, and then he and his wife might even try to take the baby away from me. After all, by that time, he would have a college degree and I would not.

B.   The next option was for my parents to adopt and raise the baby as their own. But that option was quickly snuffed out. I could not imagine my child being raised as my sibling. That would be just too weird. There was no way I could release the role of parenting completely to my parents so I crossed Option B off the list immediately.

C.   Option C was for me to move out of state with Bryan when he left for school. I could go to the local community college and try to raise the baby while having Bryan as a part-time dad. But that didn't sound too fun; raising a baby, basically on my own, leaving my parents with the knowledge that I chose Bryan over them.

D.   Option D was the option I ALWAYS thought every teen mom should choose … that is, until I was a teen mom myself. Every time I heard of someone getting pregnant, I would gladly offer up my opinion: "They should just give that baby up for adoption. That's the best option for the baby!" But after I got pregnant, I realized how much easier that kind of thing is to say when it's not your baby and not your life. Just think about how strange that sounds. You spend nine long months growing your own flesh and blood inside you, and then simply give your baby away to someone else? Let your own baby call someone else Mommy? Run the risk of never seeing your baby again? Allow him or her to live and grow up in someone else's home? Now that sounds fun, right? Option D was definitely the worst option for Lindsay Pepin, but as I looked at the other three options, it was probably the best choice for my baby. I knew that if I truly loved my child, I would want him or her to have a father, a stable, happy, nurturing and functional home, a home that could provide everything in life and then some, a mom who had actually PLANNED to welcome a baby into her life, and a mom who didn't have the word "TEEN" in her age.

The Dreaded Option D

As I stewed on the four options, it was Option D that kept coming back to the surface. But how could I select an option filled with so much personal pain? Logically I knew that this was the best option for my baby

… but what about me? Yes, the nine months of the pregnancy would be tough, but I wanted the prize at the end! On top of all this, what would the child think? How could I ensure that my baby knew that he or she was ALWAYS loved from the very beginning, that I ALWAYS wanted to keep him or her, and that I ALWAYS wanted what was best for him or her?

Logically I knew it was the right choice, but emotionally I couldn't fathom giving this child away to someone else. How could I live knowing my child would take its first steps in someone else's home? My child would cry out to another woman the first time his or her feelings got hurt. He or she would get married, and I wouldn't be the Mother of the Bride or Mother of the Groom. It was so hard for me to imagine giving up the one thing I was fighting so hard for day in and day out.

In my counseling sessions I was constantly being told that this was our choice to make, and that it had to be my choice or else I would grow to regret it and resent those who I thought had made the choice for me. But how could I make this impossible decision? My parents always said that I was a smart girl and that I heard from the Lord. But during this season of my life, that's just not where my head was. In my mind, I was thinking, *"Hear from the Lord? What? Are you missing something here? I am having a teen pregnancy! I had sex before marriage, HELLO!"* Then Satan's lies would pile on top of my own doubts. "God doesn't want to help you with this mess that you got YOURSELF into. Look at you, covered in shame and guilt. YOU'RE ALL ALONE!"

Those lies from the enemy would constantly ring in my head. Since telling my parents about the pregnancy, I hadn't prayed to God once in the four-month span. Not a single prayer came out of my mouth. During that time I was too ashamed to call upon Jesus. I thought of myself as too dirty to approach the Lord, unworthy of praying anything to Him. Before getting pregnant, I knew Jesus and prayed a lot, but that was when I didn't think I needed saving. I thought I already had it all figured out. But now that I needed saving, I felt like I was unworthy of even asking for help.

I felt like I didn't deserve the grace He so freely wanted to give. But that kind of thinking goes against the very definition of grace. Grace is God's unmerited favor. We deserve to pay for our sins, but God doesn't give us what we deserve! God forgives us and He forgets our sins forever. But I didn't understand grace at the time. I felt like God had to turn His face away from me, just like I had done to Him. I was three years old when I invited Jesus to live in my heart, and since that time, I believed fully that God had saved me, loved me, and wanted to be my friend forever. These were the truths I had believed and counted on for the last 15 years.

But as I was on my way to hitting rock bottom, covered and consumed in my own shame, guilt, and pain, I could not accept God's grace. I just couldn't see Him as Someone who could love me and accept me uncon- ditionally. How could I ask Him to bail me out when I was the one who ran so far away from Him? How could I come back to His wide-open arms when I was holding on to so much pain? How could I ask Him to remove this pain when I was the one who had put myself into this situa- tion? How could I crawl back?

Of course I had a complete misconception of God and the role He was playing in my life at the time. I was so wrapped up in my shame that I thought of God, sitting high on His throne, looking down at me, filthy and dirty because of my selfish actions. I imagined Him with His arms crossed, looking down, not in love but in judgment, waiting on me to plead for His mercy and forgiveness. He was ashamed of me, offended by my very presence. I had disappointed Him.

But that image is straight from the pit of hell. It's a lie from the devil. The truth is that God is love. God is not full of rejection and judgment.

He is LOVE, and the Bible says in 1 Peter 4:8, "Love covers over a multitude of sins." His love covers our sins completely and washes us white as snow. We're no longer filthy and undeserving. We are His children, children He loves unconditionally.

Now I imagine a completely different scenario. I crawl back before God's throne, my head held low in shame. But God, just like it says in Psalm 3:3, gently takes my chin in His loving hands and lifts it up so I can look at Him in the face. He tenderly brushes the hair back from my eyes so that I can see Him fully. But what I see surprises me. I don't see His eyes full of vengeance and judgment, but rather burning with love, love for me. In that intimate moment, my shame simply melts away and disappears forever. Finally understanding God's grace was the truth that brought me freedom.

CHAPTER 12

Lindsay

IT'S A GIRL!

As soon as adoption became a serious option, I knew I NEEDED Jesus. I was now walking in the "Major Events" category of life! I knew that if I had to walk through this adoption alone and in my own strength I would die. I don't mean that figuratively. I honestly believe that trying to function daily while having to deal with the constant feelings of desperation, depression, and pain would have killed me. I was done; I had no more fight left in me.

So I crawled to the cross of Jesus, too weak to stand, and surrendered to Him. But in the midst of all this turmoil, I had to relearn how to pray again, even though I'd been a Christian for 15 years. In many ways, I was still just a spiritual baby. For the first time in my life, I knew I needed a Savior. At this point I was so weak and ashamed that whenever I tried to pray, I couldn't find the words. All I could say was "Jesus." That was it, but that simple word carried so much meaning for me.

I would say His name over and over, and I could visualize all my cares being placed at the foot of the cross. I would say His name, and I knew He was right there next to me. I knew He was going to take care of me and the impossible situation I was in. I went a solid month just saying that single word every time I prayed, "JESUS."

I was so lost and desperate that as I lay in my bed, sobbing, the only words that would come were ... "JESUS! JESUS! JESUS!" I would wail His name out loud, in so much pain, because I knew I was going to lose my baby. Nothing but His name came from my lips, but He heard my surrendered cry. I knew that when I said His name what He heard was, "I am sorry. I have sinned. I need Your help. Give me direction. Take this pain away from me." The God of the Universe heard my cry and knew my sorrow. He held me in His presence, and He cried with me when all I could say was "Jesus." He saw through my dirty rags. I knew my only hope was Him. When my world was falling apart and I was about to lose my child, all I had to say was "Jesus."

The week had finally come. My pregnancy was halfway over! I was about to find out the gender of this baby that had been in my tummy for the last 20 weeks. Although I thought it was a boy, I was hoping it would be a girl.

I just thought that a little girl might want to get to know me as she grew older. She might want to know the whole story. She might actually care about me and want to be my friend. But I didn't think I'd have a girl so I began to prepare my heart for a little boy. I thought that with my luck, I'd have a little boy who probably wouldn't care anything about me.

The Big Reveal!

On the day of the doctor's appointment, Bryan and I walked out of school with two of his teammates. We were all joking around and just enjoying being teenagers. They wanted to go eat at Coney Islanders that day, like we usually did after school. But that day we had to come up with a quick excuse as to why we couldn't go eat with them.

Bryan and I were both excited. Since my last ultrasound many weeks before, I was finally going to be able to see my baby again. I couldn't wait to see how my baby had grown and developed over the last few months. Not only was I going to be able to see my baby, I was going to find out if it was a boy or a girl!

Bryan and I drove down to the doctor's office and went straight to the ultrasound room. This was going to be Bryan's first time to see the baby. As the ultrasound began, we were both so excited. We could see its profile, fingers, and toes! I was thrilled to see the baby move around!

On the ultrasound machine I could see the four chambers of the heart while the technician measured it. The baby's heart was beating so fast. I could hear the joyful swooshing noise. This was a baby! I couldn't stop smiling!

A beautiful life, living with a beating heart, was inside of me! It was a life being formed and created. My baby was perfection. I was so madly in love with that baby! That baby could do no wrong, that baby was perfect. I was overwhelmed with a mother's love.

This was becoming so real for me. For the first time during the pregnancy I finally understood that this baby was not a sin. It was clear to me now that getting pregnant wasn't a sin. This baby was God's way of turning my mess into something good!

The technician went on to print tons of pictures of the baby. I couldn't thank her enough because, after all, these were the only pictures of my baby that I would ever get where I was its mother. I got several pictures of the baby's cute little face. The baby loved to hold its little hands up by its face the whole time.

The technician was busy with the camera trying to get the best possible angle to determine whether the baby was a boy or a girl. She paused it right where the legs were opened and sure enough … it was a GIRL! I couldn't stop smiling. I was so happy to be having a little girl!

We walked out of the exam room and into the hallway. My heart was overflowing with joy! I couldn't stop smiling! Next, we went up to the doctor's office, happy as could be. But we were still a little nervous because the technician never gave us any feedback on how the baby was doing. I had no clue what all those measurements meant.

We went in to talk to the doctor and were relieved when she congratulated us on the baby girl and told us the good news that she was perfectly healthy! I could not have been happier!

Telling My Mom

Afterwards, I knew I needed to come up with a creative way to tell my parents. I felt that it was about time we experienced a little joy with this whole situation! My mom called me right after the appointment to see how it went. But I wanted to surprise her so I came up with a story about how the technician had trouble getting the baby in the right position to be able to determine the gender.

Then I went to Walmart to try to find an exciting way to tell my family. I was going up and down the aisles trying to think of just the right way to tell them when I realized that in my family every celebration needed food. So I made my way over to the bakery section and bought some sugar cookies with thick pink icing. Then I went over to the baby department and bought a little pink onesie in a newborn size.

I got home and tried to act normal until my dad got home, but there was no way I could wait that long! It was so hard not to just blurt out the truth to my momma. Finally, I couldn't take it any more. I went into our downstairs bathroom and got the onesie out of my purse and slowly walked into the kitchen where my mom and Gabrielle were talking. I held up the onesie in front of my shirt and said with a huge grin on my face, "Hey, Mom. Do I look pregnant in this shirt?"

"Hang on, Lindsay." She was finishing telling Gabrielle something. I don't think she even heard what I said. So I just stood there with a huge stupid grin on my face holding the pink onesie under my chin until she was finished talking to Gabrielle. My mom finally turned around to look at me.

She was shocked! She gave almost the same reaction she gave when she found out that I was pregnant. She yelled, "NO!" But this time her reaction was full of joy and not pain. In a laughing voice she yelled, "I figured you knew what it was! Aw, this is so exciting!" All three of us were so happy. Our joy was pure because regardless of how the pregnancy occurred, we all knew we were going to have a beautiful, perfect baby girl, who was already loved so much.

Surprising My Dad

Now I had some help coming up with a way to surprise my dad when he got home. As we were trying to figure out what to do, we heard the garage door start to open so we quickly decided to hang the pink onesie up in his closet with all of his t-shirts. We all knew that my dad is a creature of habit, and the first thing he does every day after work is go to his closet and change his clothes.

So I ran to the bedroom and hung the onesie in his closet, but I immediately realized that this tiny little six inch onesie would get lost in his extra large men's t-shirts. So I took it back out and just hung it on the doorknob to his closet door. While I was doing that, my mom went out to the garage and distracted him to give me more time.

When he came in the house, the first thing he asked about was the doctor's appointment. I tried the whole bit about how we didn't know yet, but I I could tell he knew something was up because none of us could hide the excitement in our voices.

We all followed my dad as he made his way back to his room. He just glanced at the onesie like it was no big deal. He opened his closet door. Then he closed the door again to give the onesie a closer look. He took it off the doorknob, and we yelled, "It's a girl!" He gave an excited, "Aww!" Then he said, "That seems like the only type of baby our family can make!"

We were excited and ate the cookies in celebration. We were all smiling, but this time our smiles were genuine … not made up. There was so much joy in our house that night. It felt like someone had let in a ray of sunlight. Of course, that "someone" was a little baby girl.

CHAPTER 13

Scarlet

PRAYING FOR GOD'S BEST FOR MY GRANDDAUGHTER

A girl! A girl! A girl! One day soon I would get to hold my precious granddaughter. I wondered what she would look like. Probably brown eyes since Bryan and Lindsay both had brown eyes. What about her personality? Her destiny? What would her childhood be like? There were so many unknowns in this equation, but one thing I knew for sure is that she would have a praying biological family lifting her up before God every day for the rest of her life. Even though I might never be allowed to be the grandmother I had always dreamt of being, there would be no other person on the planet who could fulfill the role of her biological maternal grandmother except me. This precious girl would share my DNA and whether she ever knew it or not, I was committed to be the one on my knees for her in prayer. If Lindsay chose adoption, one of my biggest prayers was that somehow and some way the adoptive parents would allow me to be in this precious baby's life.

Lindsay—New Pressures

Now that I knew the baby's gender, I knew I was going to have to make a decision about what to do very soon. It was time for me to start looking for families, so I contacted CPO and told them that I was looking to place my baby. They asked me some basic questions about what I would want to see in an adoptive family.

Bryan and I had both talked about this subject quite a bit, but the more we talked about it, the more I felt like I was going to be the one to make the final decision. When I thought about the subject of an adoptive family, there were so many things to consider. But there were a few major points that seemed to rise to the surface. First of all, I wanted my baby to have young parents so they would be able to actively play with the child. Next, I wanted the adoptive parents to have no other children or maybe just one other child so my child would feel special. I also wanted the parents to live close to me so I could see my child often. And finally, I wanted the adoptive couple to have similar coloring as Bryan and me so the child wasn't constantly being asked, "Are you adopted?"

But my most important request was that I wanted the adoptive parents to love the Lord with all their hearts and to go to the same type of church I went to. I wanted my child to be raised with similar spiritual values. I also wanted them to really desire an open adoption. I wanted them to be absolutely sure about this because I didn't want them second-guessing their decision in any way. I knew I was going to be the kind of birth mother who wanted to be able to see my baby a lot and would be asking to see pictures nonstop.

I was asked once, "How close is too close for the adoptive family to live by you?" I said, "I'd love it if they lived in my backyard!" Honestly, at the end of the day I wanted the adoptive parents to be just like the parent I hoped to be some day. Deep down, I wanted to raise the baby myself, but

I knew that wasn't an option, so the next best thing I could do was find someone who was almost a copy of me!

An Impossible Choice

CPO helped set up a meeting for Bryan and me to come to the office and look at prospective parents' books. In these books, people told all about themselves, their families, their lifestyle, and why they wanted to adopt. Every page was filled with pictures. The folks at CPO brought in a stack of about 12 of these books from families that fit within the criteria that we had previously set or at least the families came really close. As we sat in the room looking through the pages, I can barely remember the specific details about the day, it was all so surreal. I was in shock about what I was about to do.

I knew that this is the way most birth mothers picked adoptive families, but it just didn't feel to me like a natural way to do it. It was like I was handed a note that said, "Congratulations! You have a child's full life in your hands. Now you must choose the child's fate. You will choose her socioeconomic status, you will choose her religious views, you will choose the number of siblings she will have, and you will choose her parents' lifestyle. Oh … and don't screw this up or this child could grow up to hate you. But no pressure, this decision will only affect THE REST OF HER LIFE!"

As I think back on this memory, I don't remember if the CPO lady stayed in the room or not. I don't remember whether or not I said a word to Bryan. I just remember being focused on those books, reading every word and taking in every detail of every picture on every page. It was like I was studying for the biggest exam of my life, and I was not going to miss a single thing.

After looking through all of them, we were told that the next step was to meet any of the families we wanted to. I remember sitting there thinking,

"Is this all there is?" None of the families in the books felt right to me. It didn't seem like any of them would get the big green checkmark. None of them felt like, "YES! THIS IS THE FAMILY!"

In the end, I did pick four books and took them home to show to my family. As luck would have it, another girl was thinking about choosing the family we considered our favorite; and our second favorite family was thinking about moving to Arizona. There was no way I was going to give my little girl to a family moving so far away.

I remember showing the books to my family, and the process hit them funny too. It felt like none of them were like us. I just kept hoping that I'd pick up a book and my name would magically appear right there on the front cover. A book like that one would be an easy one to pick! We kept the books for about a week, but finally returned them all and told CPO that we wanted to wait on meeting the families so we could think about it some more. They told us not to get discouraged; they get new families in all the time.

The Birthing Class

That weekend, I took a free birthing class offered by CPO for expecting mothers. I was nowhere near ready to give birth, but this class was the only one they offered before my due date. On the morning of the class, I was very nervous. I wasn't sure what to expect, and I wasn't mentally prepared to even think about giving birth. I wasn't ready emotionally either. I knew very well that giving birth also meant giving up my baby.

We were told to bring along the one person we knew would be in the delivery room during the birth, so I decided to take my mom to the birthing class with me.

When we showed up in the parking lot, it was dark and rainy outside—which fit my mood perfectly. I wasn't really feeling this class, but we got out of the car and went in despite my feelings. There ended up being just four girls in the class; three of us were due around the same time. We were all about the same age, and we were all planning on placing our babies for adoption. I'm not sure I ever heard what the story was with the fourth girl, but it seemed like she was going to be keeping her baby.

As my mom and I looked around the room, we saw four GIRLS who looked like they were fighting a war. It wasn't obvious yet that any of us were pregnant, but the exhaustion and fear were written on all our faces and the faces of the people who came with us looked much the same way; their expressions seemed to all be asking, "How in the world did we get into this mess?"

This class was all about the process of having a baby. The instructor told us what would happen and how to know when we should go to the hospital. This was a lot of information for me to absorb, and I was scared that I wouldn't know what to do when the time came. But my wonderful mom was sitting right there next to me, taking notes the whole time just in case we forgot anything.

We watched videos of a birth, which confirmed to me that I wanted an epidural! After the class I just felt weird. My belly wasn't even showing yet. The whole thing was surreal and hard for me to grasp. But looking back now, I realize that God was preparing me for what lay ahead.

God will often prepare us now for something that will happen in the future. Whether it's a good thing or a bad thing, God knows the things coming up in our future, and He gently guides us in preparation so we'll be ready when the time comes. My earthly father loved me enough to make sure I did my algebra homework. He wanted me to be ready when test time came around. It just makes sense that my Heavenly Father would do the same thing. He loves us enough to make sure we're ready.

But often things in life take their own sweet time, and it's hard to be patient. Like a student watching the clock take forever for the bell to ring, it seems like the more we want time to go by quickly, the slower time seems to pass. But God has a purpose in our waiting. He uses that time to prepare us for what's up ahead.

We tend to think about time spent waiting as wasted time. But I think that's the wrong way to think about it. There are two ways to think about waiting. One way is when we're "waiting" for something to happen. But there's another way. When someone serves your table at a restaurant, that person is called waitress or waiter. During those difficult waiting times in the process, I believe God wants us to wait on Him like a waiter serves people in a restaurant. When we spend our waiting time serving Him and His Kingdom, He can do the work of preparing us for what's coming.

Thankfully God's timing is always perfect. While we are waiting, God is giving us the tools we need to receive and use the amazing gift He has for us. He could be preparing us for a fight. He might be strengthening our muscles because He knows the enemy will oppose us. He prepares us so we can do more than we could ever imagine.

I would rather wait for His timing and be prepared than to rush the process and not be ready. Just like a baby being formed in the womb, you can't rush it. I was a scared girl, 20 weeks pregnant, and no belly to show for it yet. But thankfully, I still had 20 more weeks to prepare. God's timing is always better than ours.

Scarlet

On my daughter's bed, I would never have expected, in my wildest dreams, to see photo books of smiling families hoping to be selected to raise my granddaughter. But here we were, sitting together, going through these books. I wondered how it must have felt for these couples to put their very best foot forward, presenting themselves on paper in a way that a distraught hormonal teenager might choose them as parents for her unborn child.

How was a girl Lindsay's age supposed to make such a difficult decision? Yet as I watched her work through her heart's cry for her child, I realized that this was no longer my little girl. No, my Lindsay was a woman. I marveled at the strong maternal force that continued to propel her forward to make the most selfless decision of her life.

As I sat there next to Lindsay in the CPO labor training, I couldn't help but remember back twenty years earlier when I attended my own birthing classes. I was happily married with the plan that I could stay home full time with my child. My situation could not have seemed more secure, and yet as a first-time mother I was extremely anxious as I heard about preparing for labor. Now, I couldn't imagine what Lindsay must be feeling. I found myself constantly wanting to ask her how she was doing, what she was thinking, and what her plan was.

Once again, I had to bite my tongue. I did my best to help where I could and refrain from acting like I had any idea at all what she must be going through. Oh sure, I had gone through labor before but I was able to bring my babies home with me. As this story unfolded I was in awe of the strength Lindsay possessed as she continued to choose her daughter over herself.

I was realizing that Lindsay was no longer my bright-eyed second grader in her Brownie Girl Scout uniform. No, now she was a fellow mother. Time and time again a good mother has to choose what she believes is best for her child, even when it requires a huge sacrifice. Lindsay was about to make a decision that was very adult. I was in the presence of a fellow woman for whom I was gaining a lot of respect.

CHAPTER 14

Lindsay

THE ANDERSONS

The day after returning the books to CPO, I was at a Student Council event, wearing my baggy student council shirt and a too-tight pair of shorts. It was after lunch, and people were playing basketball in the gym before the next event took place.

I sat off to the side checking my email and noticed that I had an email in my inbox from CPO. The email said that they had a new family, the Andersons, who had just applied but had not had a chance to create a book yet. The email went on to say that the Andersons fit all of our qualifications to a tee. They were young with no kids. I opened up the pictures that were attached to the email and they looked great! They also had two cute dogs. Now this was more like it. People who seemed normal … much more like me than some of the other families I'd seen. I started to feel like there could be some hope that everything would turn out okay.

I texted Bryan and had him come into the gym and eat with me so I could tell him about the email. I showed him the Andersons' picture, and we even Googled their address and found out that they were only about 20 minutes away. The rest of the day I just kept looking at their pictures and feeling better and better about them. After school, I told the lady at CPO that we were up for meeting with them. We did this on a whim, without knowing any more information about them except for their pictures, their occupations, and where they lived, but somehow it just felt right.

A Date with the Andersons

Later that day I found out that the Andersons were interested in meeting us too. We set up a date to go to dinner with them. CPO had a system for how these kinds of "open adoption" meetings would go. It was important for us to meet and make sure we would all be a good fit because we could be in each other's lives forever. Plus, everyone has a different definition of how open the adoption should be, and these meetings were a good time to make sure everyone was on the same page.

I got dressed that night feeling like I was dressing for a date. I was so nervous, probably the most nervous I'd ever been in my life. I decided to wear a black dress, and Bryan wore a collared shirt. The last thing we wanted them to think was that this baby was coming from a rough birth family.

Bryan and I got to the restaurant about 10 minutes early, and we sat in the car and thought about how this meeting could change our lives forever. We talked about what we thought the couple would be like. We got out of the car when we saw the lady from CPO pull into the parking lot. She was going to join us for dinner. Her role would be our facilitator, making sure the conversation flowed and that everyone felt comfortable.

When the Andersons showed up, they looked just as nervous as we did, but my first impression of them was very good. They seemed so nice and NORMAL. Mrs. Anderson was so happy, and she giggled a bunch while Mr. Anderson looked very manly and had a strong presence.

I was very glad the woman from CPO was there; she helped our conversation flow. We asked them questions about their jobs and their hobbies, and we told them things about our lives. I told them that we knew that the baby was a girl, but I couldn't tell if the news made them excited or not. I was so nervous the whole time, I could barely eat a thing. The night ended really well, and we all exchanged numbers so we could stay in touch.

Bryan and I were both very excited and agreed that we liked them a bunch. We went to a local ice cream shop, then drove to a Walgreen's parking lot near my house to eat our ice cream and talk about the evening. We discussed all the pros and cons of placing our baby with the Andersons and, of course, we thought of several more questions to ask them. Like most of our conversations, we ended up talking about the baby. We were feeling really good.

This was one of those moments where I felt the calm in the middle of the storm. I was starting to see signs of hope—signs that things could actually work out well. Bryan and I talked about whether I should text Mrs. Anderson to make plans to meet again, or if we should just wait on them to text us. It was crazy … it felt like we were dating! Adoption was definitely feeling like the right thing to do.

Another Date with the Andersons

Within 24 hours, Mrs. Anderson texted me saying that they'd had a good time with us and wanted to meet again. I quickly texted her back and told her that we'd had a good time too. We made plans to meet the following week for dinner again.

When Bryan picked me up for dinner that night, I immediately started crying. My emotions were all over the place. We'd felt good about the Andersons initially, but now I could tell in my gut that I didn't have peace about the situation. I hated that my mind wasn't settled, but I didn't know what else to do … but cry. We'd been so busy that day, and this was the first time I'd really had to think about what we were going to do. All my pregnant emotions were going crazy! I just couldn't calm down. My mind was making up crazy scenarios about the Andersons, wondering whether or not they would even let us see our baby again. Bryan finally calmed me down and reminded me of all the things I originally loved about them and how we hadn't made any commitments yet; this was just dinner.

Once I gained my composure, we made it to the restaurant, showing up just a little late. This time the questions got deeper on both sides. We asked them more about their religious beliefs, schooling, plans for more kids, and what the completed picture might look like. The only thing that threw up a red flag was when we got around to the subject of church.

They said that they were "hit and miss" with church and hadn't made it yet that year, even to special services like Christmas or Easter. This was so foreign to me ... church had always been such a big deal in my family. I know that salvation has nothing to do with church attendance, but I knew I wanted my baby to go as often as possible so she could consistently learn about Jesus. We continued to have a good conversation, and other than when we talked about church, everything seemed perfect. They showed us some more photos, which included pictures of their house, which was very nice.

Time for Our Parents to Meet the Andersons

After that second "date" with the Andersons, Bryan and I decided that it was time for them to meet our parents. We thought that it would be best for them to meet each set of parents separately. So the following week, the Andersons came to my house. Bryan wasn't able to make it that time. We had cookies and coffee served around the kitchen island. My dad shared with Mr. Anderson his heart and feelings about my pregnancy and future adoption. He tried to go deep and really get to know Mr. Anderson; he wanted to know what kind of man he was, and tried to get a good read on his character, faith, values, and beliefs. Most of all, he was trying to figure out what kind of father Mr. Anderson would be to his granddaughter.

Meanwhile, my mom talked to Mrs. Anderson about girly stuff like prom and high school. Then we all moved into the living room and sat down for a couple more hours and talked together. I tried really hard to let my guard down so they could see who I really was, but I just couldn't be "100 percent Lindsay" because I didn't want to let them in yet. It was too early to be sure that they were the right couple to raise my baby. How could I be 100 percent myself when I didn't even know if they were the right people to raise the most precious piece of my life?

Not only that, but how could I be 100 percent myself when I really didn't know who I was anymore? The pregnancy had thrown everything in me off. I used to be confident and sure of myself, but now I was anything but confident. Talk about an identity crisis. Was I a teenager or an adult? Was I a high school student or a young mother-to-be? I guess, in a way, I was all those things. But at the time, there's no way I could've articulated that to the Andersons.

Mr. Anderson said that he hoped that they would be able to adopt a baby girl. This gave me some assurance that at least they weren't disappointed that my baby was a girl. After about four hours, it came time for them to leave but before they left, Mrs. Anderson asked if she could see my belly because I wasn't showing yet in my clothes. She was really excited when I lifted my shirt so she could see how round my belly was becoming.

CHAPTER 15

Scarlet

GOD'S PEACE OVERCAME MY FEARS

*T*his is extremely weird, I kept thinking as I frantically swept my kitchen floor in preparation for the Andersons' visit. *How did we get here? Would I soon be meeting the parents who would be raising our grandchild?* I was focused to make sure everything looked perfect. It was so important for me that these people see that we were clean and safe and that we could be trusted to spend time with our granddaughter in the future. Dark thoughts pushed their way into my mind. *What if they just lie to us and agree to an open adoption, but in reality, have no intention of including us? What if they just shut us out?*

During the first two "dates" that Lindsay had been on with the Andersons, Brad and I had been waiting to hear every detail the minute she arrived home. Everything in me wished that I could've sat in the booth next to theirs at the restaurant allowing me to secretly eavesdrop on their conversation. I was jealous that Lindsay hadn't rushed straight home to discuss everything with me, to get my input. No, instead she sat in a car in a parking lot, discussing it all with Bryan. I shook those thoughts out of my mind. I reminded myself that this wasn't my choice to make. The reality hit me hard; this had to be Bryan and Lindsay's decision.

Now it was the third meeting, and I was finally invited to weigh in. We were going to have the chance to meet the Andersons for ourselves. As we sat across the table from the kind and attractive couple, I couldn't help but wonder what kind of atmosphere our child would grow up in. I know I shouldn't refer to the baby as "our child," but the fact is, my heart felt that she was mine too. Would these parents put Jesus as the number one voice in their home? Would they raise this baby the same way I had raised my girls? Would they parent the way I did?

As soon as that question crossed my mind, I felt the insecurities and doubts about my own ability to parent a daughter. Here I sat with a pregnant high schooler. What claim could I make on perfect parenting?

But the strange thing is, I knew that if I had the chance to parent all over again, I would parent the very same way. And yet, even though I felt like we'd done the best parenting job we knew to do, here we were face-to-face with a couple we'd just met, wondering if they were to be the ones to raise our teenager's daughter.

From the beginning of the pregnancy, I felt that one of my most important roles was to help get this precious baby to the family that God destined her to be with. It was as if I had been handed a baby at one end of a battlefield. My assignment was to deliver the baby safely into the arms of her forever mother, who was standing all the way on the other side of the battlefield with bombs and explosions going off all around, explosions of emotions, frustrations, and confusion.

I just wanted to duck my head, hold onto the baby tightly, and run as hard and as fast as I could. I may not have been physically pregnant with this baby but in my heart and spirit I was carrying her and Lindsay in prayer. *Who God? Who is supposed to raise this loved child?*

Later that night, after the visit from the Andersons, Brad and I lay side by side in the dark. "Well, what'cha think?" I whispered, as the sound of the ceiling fan set a steady clicking tempo.

Brad paused a beat and said, "They seem nice, but it's not like we're getting a Pepin Boy." "Pepin Boy" was our family's term for Brad's seven brothers, men who were steady, kind, and full of gentle integrity. I knew exactly what kind of man he was referring to. I knew because I had the honor to be married to a "Pepin Boy" myself.

Lindsay—A Difficult Decision. But the Right Decision

The next night my parents and I finally got to discuss the meeting we'd had with the Andersons. My parents were honest and expressed their reservations with me, but they made sure I knew that ultimately the choice was up to me. There are times in life when you can no longer run to Mom and Dad no matter how much you may want to. No one else can make your decisions for you. You just have to pray and then make your decision, trusting that Christ knows what's best.

The following morning, I went downstairs before school and found my mom crying. Through many tears she said, "I don't know if I'll ever get to see our baby again. How do we know that they aren't lying to us? I want to be her grandma! I want her to grow up in church, listening to Bible stories."

She was so upset and crying so hard! I was a little concerned about her strong emotional reaction. I kept asking her, "Is it the Andersons that you don't like, or is it the decision to put the baby up for adoption that you don't like?" She didn't seem to know the answer. She just kept sobbing, and I did my best to console her while trying to make sense of it all.

Was her anxiety caused by the Andersons specifically or adoption in general? That was the big question. If she was having a hard time with adoption in general, she might struggle no matter which family we picked. But if it was the Andersons, I needed to know. We were close to making the decision. I trusted my mom's judgment; her opinion mattered to me. I left for school that day with all this weighing heavily on my mind.

As the school day passed, I started to feel the very same way my mom was feeling. And over the course of the week, my peace slowly ebbed away. By the end of the week, I no longer felt good about the Andersons adopting my baby. Looking back, I think I had known this in my heart since we'd met with them the second time. It was hard to sort through all my emotions while having so much on my mind. But now it was time for me to stand my ground. This baby was mine, and I felt that it was my responsibility to make sure the right decision was made.

Fortunately, I didn't have to be the one to make the difficult phone call to Mrs. Anderson. The lady from CPO called me to ask how I was feeling about the Andersons, and I told her that we'd decided that they weren't going to be a good fit. There was nothing truly wrong with them. I was sure they were great people, and I had no doubts that they loved the Lord very much. I just knew my baby wasn't supposed to be theirs; it's as simple as that.

Sometimes we can want something so bad without realizing that what God has for us is so much better. "Good" isn't always God's best. He already has a plan mapped out for us, a plan filled with blessings. Like the saying goes, "Some of God's greatest gifts are unanswered prayers." Today, I'm sure the Andersons would agree. They have since adopted a very cute little boy. Our decision ended up being God's best for them as well.

Scarlet

I couldn't stop crying. How does someone make a decision like this? You could line up hundreds of couples and go through checklist after checklist trying to get just the right set of parents but in the end, how could one truly be sure that you've chosen correctly? Most babies don't get to choose in which family they will be born. For better or for worse they are stuck with the people who bring them home from the hospital.

Here we were in the midst of what seemed to be an impossible situation, helping to choose what this baby's life would be. I knew that no one could know the future; ultimately only God knew what would be best for this baby. Were we going to be able to trust that He could guide us? Many sleepless nights had been part of this journey, but on this morning the enormity of the decision settled heavily on my shoulders. I couldn't help but think that we were in way over our heads. I felt that we were ill-equipped to make such a huge, important decision. My mind was overwhelmed and my emotions were running a 100 miles per hour.

Lindsay walked through the family room on her way out the front door to go to school. I felt like she walked in on me as I was throwing a youngster's temper tantrum before God. The last thing I wanted to do was weigh Lindsay down with even more pressure, but here I was emotionally dredging up all my angst.

I knew that Lindsay looked to me and valued my input. As much as we kept telling her that this was her decision, I wondered if one day my grandchild would wonder why I didn't step in to cast a different vote. A "vote"; that's crazy! How in the world can one person possibly cast a vote that will affect someone else's life?

But isn't that always the case? We all make decisions, both for good and bad, that influence and even direct the lives of others. That's the benefit of strong families and strong communities. Each of our lives are interconnected with the lives of others. This is what holds us close and keeps us secure. Our positive choices can positively affect and bless the lives of others.

But the opposite is also true. Our negative choices can have far-reaching effects on those we are closest to.

Think of it like the game of Jenga. Our lives, like those little blocks of wood, are all stacked and connected with other lives around us. We can't just simply pull one block out and expect that there will be no effect on the stack. A problem with one block will often lead to problems with the other blocks, making them vulnerable to a big crash.

The fact is our actions do affect the lives of others. And on that Thursday morning, I felt the weight of the decision we were faced with—a decision in which this precious child would have absolutely no say.

As Lindsay closed the door and headed out to face another long day at school, I sensed a peace come over the room. In that quiet moment, I knew that God was with us, and that He would lead us to the right parents for this baby.

All along this journey the Lord surprised us time and time again with these quiet, peaceful moments. The storm may have still been raging, but it's as if Jesus held up His hands and simply said, "Peace, be still." In those precious moments, I felt that I had crawled up into the lap of Jesus and felt His strong arms around me. I could see the look of love on His face and feel the love and protection in His arms.

Whenever this happened, I truly took it as a gift from Him. It was as if I was still a little girl, and my Heavenly Father knew exactly what I needed in that moment. He was right there to scoop me up in all my emotional frenzy and hold me close. Gradually my breathing slowed down and my heart rate matched His. I understood that in that precious place of peace there was nothing that could harm me. In that place, I knew that everything would be all right. His Word tells us that His peace passes all understanding (Philippians 4:7). So when the facts say we should be freaking out about something, the Lord just downloads His peace on us, a peace that makes no human sense. What a good and trustworthy Father He is!

CHAPTER 16

Lindsay

THE NEW NORMAL

As the weeks continued to go by, my pregnancy had become somewhat normal for my family. I was dealing with it. My parents and sisters were dealing with it. We were all settling into the fact that while life was nowhere near the "normal" we were all used to, we were at least able to accept that this had become the "new normal."

We made it all the way into April keeping the pregnancy a secret just among our immediate family, my grandparents, and a couple of very close friends we knew we could trust. Now there was a lot of discussion about when to tell the extended family on both sides. It was very hard to find an appropriate way to tell everyone when we had such a large extended family spread out over so many different places. We didn't want those we loved the most to find out from someone else.

My dad wanted to tell his side of the family when we'd all be together at an Easter lunch event. But I didn't want everyone to find out while I was standing right there in front of them. I just knew that would be extremely awkward for all of us for the rest of that day. I begged him in the car ride home from the Easter church service not to announce it at lunch. I didn't want to have to spend the rest of the day with people just looking at me in shock and pity. Thankfully, he agreed to wait a few more weeks.

It was my hope that my parents could just send an email to everybody at the same time, but my dad thought that delivering important news like that by email would be too insensitive. We finally settled on the decision that my mom would call each person on her side of the family, and my dad would tell his dad and brothers at their monthly poker game. The brothers would then tell their wives, and so on. My dad would just wait a little later to call the others in the family who were out of state. I am so grateful to have wonderful parents who were willing to step in and take on the job of telling everyone for me. I was thankful that I wasn't the one having to share the news over and over again.

Getting the word out to close friends and family was a big deal. My immediate family had been living with this news for a few months and had all gotten used to the reality that I was pregnant. But now, with the news coming out, it was going to come up all over again. My extended family was now going to hear all about my pregnancy. I was split ... 70 percent of me dreaded telling everybody, but the other 30 percent just didn't care anymore. Okay, okay, I had sex and got pregnant. I wanted to scream, "Have you ever sinned? Aren't you glad that your secret sin doesn't turn public like mine has done? But this baby is not a sin! This baby is not shame! This baby is LOVED! This baby will change the world!"

Missing Prom

People went crazy for the major social events at my school. They started talking about them and planning for them months in advance. This was especially true for prom, which was a big deal because it was for seniors only. We had all been waiting since our freshman year for this big event.

A full two months prior to prom, people started to reserve party buses and limos for the special night.

Naturally I assumed that by the time prom came, news of my pregnancy would already be out. I'd be over five months pregnant by that time, and I knew that uptight parents would be upset that there was a pregnant girl in their kid's prom pictures. Honestly, I didn't blame them. But just because I didn't blame them didn't mean I was prepared to put up with it, so I decided that it would be best if I didn't go.

But it was hard to have to listen to everyone talk nonstop about the dance. I had to repeat over and over, "No, I'm not going," which was weird because just back in September I was having the time of my life at the homecoming dance. I was normally the one right in the middle of all the dance planning. I loved the preparation and then dancing the night away at the event. School dances were my absolute favorite part of going to high school.

But now prom was right around the corner, and I still was not showing in my clothes. This little baby girl was a pro at sticking to my spine! As the date approached, I started to feel disappointed that we weren't going. I could tell that Bryan was picking up on my disappointment. The week before prom was terrible; I was in a horrible mood, crying and upset all the time. When he asked why I was so upset, I admitted to him that I just wished we'd made the decision to go to prom in the first place.

A Change of Plans

Then two nights before prom, Bryan left a message on my phone saying he thought it would be a good idea if he took me to the prom. He wanted me to know that he thought it was important for us to just be kids for the night.

I was excited to be going, but now that meant I was going to have to scramble to figure out what to wear. By now I had a baby bump that I had no trouble hiding under t-shirts, but I wasn't too sure about being able to hide it in a prom dress.

I went shopping and realized right away that I needed a very large "flowy" dress, especially since my chest was so large! My mom jumped into action and started to search everywhere for me. I remembered one of my friends from middle school who had a really fashionable older sister who was about my size. I called her and told her that Bryan had decided not to go to the spring game. He wanted to stay home and go to the prom so I was on short notice to find a dress. I asked her if she would let me try on some of her older sister's old dresses.

She told me no problem and fortunately, one of her dresses was just right. It was beautiful, fit great, and hid my bump! It was a little tight, but overall the dress fit really well! I even felt kind of pretty, which was a rare thing for a girl who was 25 weeks pregnant.

We were now in a rush to get everything put together in time for Saturday night. Bryan and I went together to get the flowers, and I hurried to the mall to get some last-minute jewelry that would go with my dress. Then we had to figure out where we were going to eat before prom, because it was too late to join any of the other groups. Our friends were all riding in full limos that night, and they had already made dinner reservations of their own. The craziness was a little bit stressful, but the details came together so quickly we didn't even have time to over think things, which was good.

For once I was able to make quick decisions. It was nice to be able to make decisions on easy things like earrings and shoes as opposed to the major life decisions I was wrestling with like who was going to raise my baby. The prom was big drama for lots of my friends, but the night was actually a relief for me. I finally had something to think about besides the baby.

A Perfect Night

Prom night was perfect, just what I needed to feel like a kid again! We took fun photos in the photo booth, danced the night away, and met up with all our friends. No one even seemed to notice my belly. Afterwards, I was exhausted! My feet were swollen, my dress fit super tight, and I was ready to get home. I was in bed by midnight and went to sleep with a smile on my face.

Thinking back on that night, it's a great reminder of how important it is to celebrate fun. I know now that anytime you're going through a tough stage in life, it's healthy to intentionally value happiness by taking the time to experience the fullness of joy. Proverbs 17:22 says, "A cheerful heart is good medicine, but a crushed spirit dries up the bones." When we are able to celebrate joy, it's like cool water to a quenched spirit. For weeks I'd been living with a dry, parched spirit. There were times I felt so brittle that I would emotionally crater at the drop of a hat. I desperately needed to experience the "good medicine" that comes from a cheerful heart. That prom night for me was healing; it was a good opportunity to put all the negative thoughts out of my head, just have fun, and laugh.

Now that prom was over, there was only a month left of high school; and I figured I would have smooth sailing all the way to summer break. I was heading back to school from an amazing night at the prom and was ready to wrap up the year. I had downloaded a baby calendar app on my phone that tracked the baby's growth by comparing the size of the baby to different kinds of fruit. I couldn't wait to check the app each week so I could see how the baby was developing.

This was one of my favorite things to look forward to. I was so in love with this precious little one and loved seeing all the amazing things that were happening to her in my belly. It was fun seeing the creation process up close. She was so special to me, and I was continually amazed at how

He was "knitting" her together in my womb (Psalm 139:13). I was able to feel just a little bit of the love that God has for each one of us.

The Bible says in Ephesians 2:10, "For we are God's handiwork, created in Christ Jesus to do good works, which God prepared in advance for us to do." Some versions even use the word "masterpiece." I definitely thought my baby was a masterpiece! I was keenly aware that God was preparing this little one to do good, maybe even great, works for His Kingdom. I was energized and maybe even a little overwhelmed with the responsibility of bringing this little one into the world.

But I also had the awareness that God had created ME to do good works as well, and this baby was definitely a "good work"! I was convinced that I was God's handiwork too, born for a purpose, created to fulfill a destiny laid out just for me. That thought alone helped to ease the feelings of guilt and shame that I continued to struggle with daily.

After prom, I looked ahead to the week of graduation, which was the next "landmark" on my horizon. It would fall during the last week of my second trimester, and I knew I was going to start getting big by then. I read that by that time, the baby would already be two pounds. I was shocked when I realized that babies were actually born that small! I was giddy with the thought that this little creature was going to go to graduation with me!

CHAPTER 17

Scarlet

A CHURCH FOR LINDSAY

One of my favorite things about the new church we were going to was that every Friday they gave away free groceries to local families who were either unemployed or in a tough spot between paychecks. We had been attending the church regularly since Lindsay had first found out she was expecting. Lindsay was our number one priority, and we wanted her to have a church where she felt that she could connect with God.

When she suggested this particular church, her explanation drew us to their location. Through tears she told us, "I just feel like if I went up to the altar during the service, and walked up to the pastor and told him that I was pregnant from premarital sex, he would say, 'Did you ask God for forgiveness?' And I would tell him yes, and he would say without any judgment, 'Okay, good; then go on back to your seat.'"

We found the church to be a group of nonjudgmental believers who welcomed all people just as they were. That was exactly the kind of openness that Lindsay's heart was drawn to.

My Religious Heart Revealed

As a pregnant teenager, it was clear that Lindsay needed a safe place. If this church was void of anything, it was religion and judgment. When we first visited, I glanced around the parking lot on the way in to the service and saw a few kids who looked pretty sketchy to me. In all my wise motherly wisdom I reported, "I don't know, Lindsay. Some of the teenagers in the youth group are ... uh ... looking like they're up to no good."

Without a hint of sarcasm, Lindsay quietly replied, "I know, Mom, and your teenager daughter is pregnant." Her words hit me right in the bull's-eye of my elitist heart. She was right, of course; my "churchie" ideas were being exposed for what they really were ... shallow and judgmental. All my years of saying and believing that we as Christians need to reach out to sinners and to those who were flawed were now being tested. My heart was unveiled, revealing a judgmental attitude that I didn't even realize I carried.

Somehow from a very young age without even knowing it I had picked up an "Us vs. Them" mentality. As I sat in church service after church service throughout my entire life, I believed that we should love everyone and lead others to Jesus, but the "others" were those who had purposely continued to make bad decisions.

Sure, I tried to help them whenever I could, but I was always careful to keep the others at arm's length so their lifestyles wouldn't somehow pull me down. Yet those were the exact people Jesus sat down with and ate with, always pointing them to His loving Father. The "others" were the people who needed a Savior. What I had yet to learn was that we are all ... "the others."

Jesus didn't condemn the others; He loved them and embraced them; it was the hypocritical religious leaders He condemned. People who thought they had their act together and thought they were better than everyone else. Those are the ones for whom Jesus saved His harshest comments.

We work so hard at keeping up a good front that we pay no attention to our own dark hearts. We think we're so much better than the others when we're actually just as flawed, just as guilty. Our thoughts, attitudes, and motives—those things others can't see—are the things Jesus wants to deal with in all of us. First Samuel 16:17 says, "The LORD does not look at the things people look at. People look at the outward appearance, but the LORD looks at the heart." People can't see your thoughts, they can't always determine your motives, but God can. He sees your heart. And that day, I saw my heart the way He saw it, and I wasn't very pleased with what I saw.

In one quick moment in that church parking lot, I wanted to drop to the asphalt in repentance ... repentance and the realization that I was one of those hypocritical religious people. I was reminded that I am a sinner saved by grace because of what Jesus did on the cross. Further, I realized that I'm not saved by the outside things that others see, like good behavior or by my checking off all the boxes. The only thing that saves me is the blood of my Savior, Jesus Christ.

Jesus' love for all mankind is full of grace and is unconditional. In the Bible, Luke 5:32, Jesus tells us that He did not come to call the righteous to repentance, but sinners. God loves all of us and sent His only Son to die for our sins on the cross so that we could be forgiven and live a life of abundance and filled with intimacy with God. We must remember that all of us have fallen short of the glory of God and need a Savior.

As a Christian I never want to forget that what is good and holy in my life is because of Jesus, and not because of any works that I have done to try to earn right standing with Him. A personal relationship with God through Jesus is what I want, not a bunch of rules and regulations.

I was gaining a whole new understanding that our churches should be drawing all men and women to a place of safety and love. As we walked across the church parking lot, I whispered a prayer to Him, "Father, forgive me."

Bringing Comfort

Every week, we were the family who walked into church with our precious pregnant teenager. We sat by her, we stood and worshipped next to her, we loved on her, and we fervently prayed for her.

Lindsay faithfully went to church each week and seemed to genuinely want to be there. We never had to force her to join us on Sundays. In fact, the only time I'd see her get uncomfortable was when the service was over. I knew she wanted to get to the car quickly, hoping to avoid seeing anyone from her school. She still wanted to keep the secret as long as she could.

I knew I could not control the timing of her announcement. This had to be on Lindsay's terms. All I could control was the role I had been given. I wanted to be there to help Lindsay any way I could and right now, that was helping her get to church every Sunday.

Lindsay's pregnancy seemed to awaken a new "mothering" instinct within me. I worked hard to make sure dinners were ready in the evenings when my family came home, weary from tackling their day. I wanted to do all I could to make our home a place of peace.

From our 14-year-old's resentment towards Lindsay to Brad's feelings of failing as a father, everyone in our home seemed to be hemorrhaging in one way or another. School was almost out, and Lindsay had still not decided who would adopt her baby.

I knew I could not make this decision for her. There's no way Brad and I would ever want her looking back on this time in her life and thinking that her parents made her give her baby away. We could pray for her and be a listening ear, but it was going to have to be her decision. I may not have known a lot, but I did know one thing, Lindsay did not want me probing by asking her a lot of questions she had no interest in answering.

Admittedly, I felt out of my element with the whole situation. The truth was, I had no workable solutions for Lindsay. It seemed like all my ideas were a swing and a miss. But I was committed to keep on swinging and trying to bring comfort any way I could.

Lindsay—The Secret Leaks Out

The Monday after prom my friend Rachel called me from work and said that one of her coworkers, who was also one of our classmates, asked if I was pregnant. I missed the call so she left the message on my voice mail. My jaw dropped! Was I starting to show that much? Were other students beginning to notice?

I was still trying to sort out important questions like who would adopt my baby, and the last thing I wanted was an audience watching my every move. People began to ask my friends questions about me. When the rumors started to spread, it's funny how no one even thought to talk to me about it. It's much more fun to talk about me to everyone BUT me!

Here I was in the eye of the storm just watching people chatting about my life, whether I was pregnant or not, and the changes going on with my body. It seems that gossip has become a second language in our culture today, especially on social media. It rolls off the tongue, or off the keyboard, as easy as saying our name. Proverbs 18:8 says, "The words of a gossip are like choice morsels; they go down to the inmost parts." To me that verse says that passing up a bit of gossip is hard; it's like passing up a cookie from the bakery counter. It looks so good you can almost taste it before it even gets to your mouth. It's kind of like when someone approaches you and says, "I heard something about your friend…." It's almost too delicious to pass up. We just have to take a bite! We just have to hear the rest of that story.

But we need to ask ourselves, would we be as quick to spread gossip if those we're talking about were standing right in front of us? Are we really that enticed by hurtful stories about other people? We need to examine closely the words that come out of our mouths. Is what we are saying beneficial to anyone? Are we spreading love or hurt with our words? The Bible says that the tongue (our words) has the power of life and death…" (Proverbs 18:21). Are we using our words to build people up or tear them down?

I am pretty sure that I was the only senior who wanted the last days of her senior year to drag on even longer. Every day that went by, I prayed for just one more day of secrecy at school before everyone found out that I was pregnant. Yet at the same time, I wanted it all to just be over. But I had fears that if everyone found out about my pregnancy, either I wouldn't be able to graduate, or I would have to miss out on walking at gradua-tion, or I might even have to take classes over the summer.

I felt like a person on death row, knowing that my execution day was coming but, in my case, I wasn't sure exactly which day it was going to be. When was the day that everyone would finally find out the truth? I lived with a constant knot in my stomach and my throat. I was so scared that people would find out my secret. I had made it to the second to last Monday. Now I only had two more weeks to go, and I would be DONE with high school forever.

But by the time the next week came around, my pregnancy was the main item of speculation around school; and they weren't just whispering behind my back anymore. People I didn't even know were trying to find out about my "status." They started talking to my friends, trying to dig up any tidbit of information they could find. They were talking to Bryan about it, and I even started to get texts from random classmates asking if

"I was okay." When the truth was, they didn't really care whether I was okay or not; they were just fishing for information. They were just after their own morsel of gossip that they could spread around.

One of the biggest gossips at school, someone who had never been one of my close friends, actually had the gall to text me and say, "Lindsay, I am always here for you, and don't forget, I am a great listening ear." UMMM WHAT? Listening ear and LOUD mouth! I kept getting texts like that from all kinds of people!

CHAPTER 18

Lindsay

ENOUGH!

'd finally had enough. Trying to keep this whole thing a secret was exhausting for both Bryan and me. So we decided to spend that week calling all our friends who were still unaware of the pregnancy and making sure they knew the truth. Bryan called his friends, and I called mine. The conversations all started the same way: "I'm sure you've heard the rumors … well … they're true. Bryan and I are doing fine, and we have decided to place the baby for adoption."

I would say the whole thing, all at once, without a pause. I didn't want to give them even a moment to reply. I knew they'd be in total shock. But in the end, I was the one in shock because all my friends were wonderful. Every single person I called was either excited for the baby or concerned with how I was doing. Not a negative word was said, except a few who had trouble understanding how I could put my baby up for adoption.

I tried to explain to them as best I could how it was the right choice for the baby, even though it may not have been what I wanted. As the week went on, I was able to build up a small little army of friends who helped us combat all the drama that swirled around us. They made sure I never had to walk anywhere in school by myself. I even felt support and protection from Bryan's friends.

My friends didn't have to stand by me in support, but they were more loyal than I could have ever imagined. When I was feeling weak, they helped me continue to be strong. None of us can be strong every time and in every area of our lives. No matter who we are, there will come a time when we're going to need those who love us to surround us and help us continue to stand. As Christians, we need to find people in our lives who will hold us up when we no longer have the strength to stand on our own. We need to find people who will pray for us when we are walking through our troubles.

Thankfully, those were the kind of friends I had. Now that my secret was out, I was no longer in isolation and that felt like walking out of a dark cave and into a brilliantly bright sunny day. It felt like freedom. The things that were hidden in the dark corners were now exposed to the light. The power of the secret had been taken away. When we can be vulnerable enough to share what we are going through with others, the light comes in and the fear and loneliness dissipate.

By Thursday of that week I had reached my breaking point. People were just assuming that everyone knew I was pregnant. To me, it felt like my pregnancy was the major topic of conversation all over school. People were making up all sorts of things about me that weren't even true. They didn't know what they were saying, talking about how I was having a baby boy and about how Bryan and I were making all kinds of plans together. They were spreading any other piece of information they thought they had "heard" as if it were the truth. But they were all lies.

I was the talk of the school, and the main thing they were talking about wasn't even the fact I was pregnant. It was the fact that I was a pregnant *Christian*. It didn't matter that the people doing the talking had already had sex with dozens of other people. All that mattered was that I was the Christian who "got caught."

One day, a loud girl, known for gossiping, took it upon herself to announce to the whole class that she knew, "Lindsay was always a closet slut. It's always the Christians who are the skanks." I just wanted to scream, "WE ALL SIN! SIN IS SIN! BEING PREGNANT ISN'T A SIN! MY BABY IS NOT A SIN! HAVING SEX BEFORE YOU GET MARRIED IS THE SIN!"

Junior Mom to the Rescue!

I put up with this kind of gossip all day long, and one night after receiving a long text from someone I didn't even know, I broke down and began to sob. My older sister, who was already home from college, did her best to console me, but I just couldn't take it anymore. I felt like there was no way I could survive my last week of high school. I was exhausted, pregnant, and tired of all the gossip. There was no way I would be able to find the courage to go to school that Friday.

My older sister Alyssa knew something needed to be done so she called my mom. I remember her words perfectly, "Mom, Lindsay cannot go to school again. She has to be done." My sister came to my rescue! She was always known in our family as "Junior Mom." She could run her own household at seven years old. Normally I hated her in my business, but it felt good to have my family standing up for me.

No More School!

All semester long I had been saving my four excused absences. At my high school, you actually have the graduation ceremony before your last day of school. But if you have enough excused absences saved up, you don't have to come back after the ceremony. I had one week and one day left until graduation; that meant just six more days. But then I still had another four days to go after the ceremony. That meant I had a total of ten days of school left. My mom agreed with Alyssa and decided that I would use one of my four excused absences that Friday, and then she would call the school and figure out where to go from there.

I attended a school with almost three thousand students in the high school, which is the size of some private universities. We had one head principal and five assistant principals to deal with the day-to-day stuff of students. We were assigned our assistant principal based on the first letter of our last name.

Wouldn't you know, my principal just so happened to be known as the principal who followed the rules to the letter. He was very strict and had no tolerance ... about anything. There was no way he was going to let me off the hook. I knew this principal a little because of all my years on student council, but I didn't think he'd know who I was.

My mom gave him a call and explained my situation. Surprisingly, he was very understanding telling my mom that he knew who I was and knew this wasn't my normal character. He was curious about how I was doing. He'd seen me around school and wanted to make sure I was eating enough. I couldn't believe it ... THIS MAN ACTUALLY CARED!

He told my mom that I did not have to attend school any longer, which was fantastic news. But he went on, telling her that I would still be able to graduate on time, getting to walk across the stage with my class at the graduation ceremony. I just had to make sure I got all my assignments done.

It was all working out, and I could finally breathe. He sent all my teachers an email saying that I had an "extreme illness" that kept me from going to class the final week.

Scarlet—The News Spreads

Whether it was at the grocery store or the dry cleaners, anytime I saw a friend that I hadn't personally called, I would force myself to approach them and see how they were doing. Then I would share my memorized line, "I'm not sure if you have heard, but our middle daughter Lindsay is pregnant." Their face would immediately tell me if they had heard or not. I was in no way trying to catch anyone in gossip because I knew that among these friends, they wouldn't talk about it at all, and if they did, they'd only be sharing it out of concern. I just wanted to put them at ease that there wasn't an "elephant in the room."

It was interesting that I rarely felt judgment from others when I told them the news of the pregnancy. But I did sense judgment when the conversation turned to adoption. Everyone seemed to have an opinion on what Lindsay should choose.

The most caring response I received was one that I hope to repeat if I'm ever with someone who is facing a controversial decision. This wise acquaintance told me, "When we heard that she had chosen adoption, I was confident that this was the best decision because I knew the people deciding were seeking God for the answer."

Gabrielle Needs Her Mother

As Lindsay's mother, I wanted to be there for her 100 percent, but at the same time, I wanted to be 100 percent available to mother Gabrielle too.

"Mommmmmm, I can't go to school anymore!" Gabrielle moaned through tears as she burst through the front door.

"What's wrong?" I quickly walked from the kitchen to the living room as her painful outcry pulled on my maternal instincts. My youngest child was in agony.

"Amanda said that Beth was telling everyone in fifth hour that my sister's pregnant." I pushed her wet curl away from her cheek. "I'm so sorry, G."

For the next twenty minutes my then eighth grader poured her heart out. She gave me the play-by-play of every detail and how she didn't know what to say and how she feared other parents wouldn't let their kids come over and spend the night.

"You know it's true, Mom. If you knew that someone's teenage sister was pregnant, you wouldn't let me spend the night with them."

I immediately remembered a time several years before when I heard about another family that had just found out that their high school daughter was pregnant. It was interesting that my first thought was, *"I wonder what's going on over there?"*

Make no mistake; parenting is hard. I couldn't dismiss or minimize the pain that Gabrielle was feeling. She was dealing with very real pain and confusion. How could I help her navigate these waters that even I was having trouble with? I held her close and did my best to comfort her and dry her tears.

We constantly want to make sure our kids are safe and make sure they all have friends who help them to be better people. We as parents need to continue to encourage one another during this journey. It is so easy to be too quick to judge someone else's parenting when we all know that every child has a free will of his own, regardless of parenting styles. God calls us to choose grace over judgment.

In this new chapter of parenting, I found myself biting my tongue and allowing Gabrielle to vent. "It's not fair. I had no choice in this. Lindsay chose it for me. The boys are going to think that I'm a slut. People are going to think that I am going to be like my sister. No one is going to know that I'm a good girl."

After the rant died down, we were able to have a conversation about forgiveness, sticking beside people, even when they've disappointed us, and how we have all made decisions that affect other people. I was able to remind Gabrielle to think of what Jesus would do in each circumstance. We also agreed that we were glad that summer break was right around the corner. With only one week of classes left, Gabrielle put on a brave face and tried to ignore the whispers of her peers.

CHAPTER 19

Lindsay

AN INTERESTING PROPOSITION

Since I no longer had to attend classes, things in my life finally started to calm down. As I waited for graduation, other things in my life were finally starting to fall into place. Earlier that same month, my extended family was informed about the pregnancy. The day after they were told, my Aunt Jana (my dad's younger sister) gave my parents a call and asked if they could meet.

My parents finally returned home after a very long talk with Jana and her husband. What makes this couple so unique is that my uncle worked for Child Protection Services, and my aunt was a counselor for troubled youth. They had plenty of experience with teen pregnancy and with children being placed in all different types of home situations. My uncle and aunt were definitely experts in this area.

During their meeting, they shared with my parents that children placed in adoptive situations typically do best when the child is put with someone in the same family and are able to have consistent contact with the birth parent(s). Their main point was that placing the child with a stranger was not always the best option. Not only did they give us this great free advice, they also offered to raise the baby themselves!

You read that right; my aunt and uncle actually offered to raise my baby. I was shocked. I was trying to process all this information, trying to figure out what the next 18 years of my life might look like. How would this affect my child, and what would my child be like in their home? My mind was going a mile a minute.

This was the first time I actually thought about their parenting style and about how they raised their kids. I thought about how this couple actually lived their lives outside the limitations of a tiny 10-page family book like the one I was shown at the adoption agency. With my aunt and uncle there would be no "what ifs" about how they would raise my daughter. I knew they would raise her in a godly home. Not only did I really know these people well, I loved them.

But it was hard to wrap my head around this new idea. I had a plan in my head that my child would go to a stranger. I even remember thinking at the beginning of this whole ordeal that the baby going to a family member was not going to be an option. But now with all this new information, I just got quiet and did my best to process this new option.

Another Interesting Proposition

The next day, my dad had a long phone call and then went out for a walk with my mom. They came back in after their walk and shared with me that my dad's younger brother, Jeff, and his wife, Bethany, had called and said that they can't imagine this baby not being in the Pepin family. My parents were downstairs and I was in the loft upstairs looking down and listening to them tell me about their phone call with Jeff.

I began to sob. I cried out, "Is there anyone ELSE who wants this baby?" It felt like people were having secret meetings regarding my life; then they would just pop up and ask for my baby. It was confusing and too much information for me to sort through. My feelings were all over the map; I felt relief and love, but I also felt shock. I felt blessed, but I also felt frustrated and confused.

There were now so many options to sort through and so many people whose feelings could get hurt. I needed extra time to think this through, so I asked my parents to tell both couples that I would wait until after graduation to make my decision. I just needed to focus on one challenge at a time.

Rehearsal for the Big Day

I may have been released from attending school, but that didn't mean people stopped talking and texting about my situation. Although we had already told our friends, unfortunately the word was still gradually trickling out to everyone else. Bryan was still going to school every day so he was the one who really had to deal with most of the questions. I was just happy to be safe at home, away from all the drama. The week had come and gone; now it was time for graduation rehearsal. It was time for reentry. I had to face the noise of all the people again.

I showed up for rehearsal with my friends and just acted like I didn't know what was going on or that anyone knew. Bryan and I had the same first letter of our last names, so we were able to sit on the same row, but we weren't placed next to each other. We were lucky, though; the teacher who was in charge of our row had been close to Bryan for many years and knew about the pregnancy. Thankfully, she switched our name cards so we could sit by each other. It was a relief to know that I would be sitting by Bryan and not some stranger who might say something rude about the pregnancy.

During rehearsal, a guy behind us said, "Oh, I have such a big problem. Do I nap or do I eat after this?" Bryan leaned over and whispered to me, "I wish that was my biggest problem." I couldn't have agreed more. It's funny how we all have a different perspective of what a "problem" is. To that guy, what to do after the rehearsal was the biggest issue in his life at the time. But to us, that was nothing. We were struggling with something we felt was far greater. But as big as our struggle was, there may have been someone even in our same row with a much greater problem, maybe they'd found out they had cancer or that a loved one had died. The fact is, we just don't know the battle the person next to us or in front of us is facing. We think our problems are the biggest ones around.

We all go through pain in life. We all experience real hurts. The only person who will ever fully understand our pain is Jesus. He's the One who bore our pain as He hung on the cross and took the blow for our sins. He knows what it's like to suffer, He knows what it's like to be falsely accused, and He knows what it's like to sacrifice Himself for someone else. That's why He's the One who can comfort us during our pain, because He's got real credibility. He's been there. He knows what it's like. We know Jesus as our Savior, but He is also our Comforter. He comes and brings us peace and comfort. And His Word says He'll never leave us or forsake us (Hebrews 13:5). He may not lift us out of the storm, but He promises to be by our side all the way through the storm, no matter how bad the storm gets.

Bryan and I made it through graduation rehearsal, and we were finally ready for the big day. I remember my mom telling me, "Someone might yell out something rude as you walk across the stage so you need to be prepared." I knew it was a possibility, but no one was going to ruin this moment for me. I was graduating high school with a 3.8 GPA, three years in student leadership, and 12 credit hours of college already completed. I had earned this.

Time to Graduate

When it comes to graduations, most students hate how ugly the big baggy gown is. But I loved it! I rode to the graduation ceremony with my wonderful friends. I was still pretty nervous, but their excitement filled the car and made me feel better. Of course, it didn't help that we were already late and had to park so far away, but I insisted on wearing my four-inch heels even though I was rocking pregnancy ankles! I had something to prove. These immature high school kids were not going to steal this moment from me.

As we rushed in we had to go through a security check. We all had to take off our graduation gowns so they could check us for anything we might use that could disrupt the ceremony. I was grateful that no one was around except my friends.

We all stood around in the large gymnasium waiting to walk out for the ceremony. Fellow students looked at me and a few even pointed, but I just kept my chin up because I knew I would never have to see these people again. I was not going to cower on my big day! I deserved this. I made it! I was graduating!

The ceremony went great! Bryan's and my parents sat together which made us feel supported. No one yelled anything as I grabbed my diploma and walked off stage in victory. Just me, and the little friend I was carrying in my belly, had made it through the ceremony and we walked across the stage together! I was now a high school graduate regardless of the fact that I was pregnant. My situation did not define me nor stop me from getting my diploma.

CHAPTER 20

Lindsay
PROS AND CONS

As the summer began, my pregnancy was becoming just that much more real to me. I had a baby inside of me that could live on its own now if it needed to. That meant I could no longer put off the question of what I would do if I had this baby today. I could no longer pretend that having a baby wasn't going to happen. I had to face the music that this child was going to be born and I needed a plan. I knew that in the heat of the moment, things might not go the way we thought. And if that happened, I would probably be emotional and that's not the best frame of mind to be making very important decisions. I needed to walk into the hospital knowing exactly what I was going to do when I walked out. It was time to make the plan. It was time for me to pick the right parents for my perfect child.

I first took a close look at both sets of relatives who offered to raise my baby, and made a "pros and cons" list. Bethany was a stay-at-home mom, with a 9-month-old baby girl. She was just eight years older than me, and I'd always known her to be a very calm, peaceful woman. But I didn't feel like she knew anything about adoption, or how to deal with this unique situation.

On the other hand, there was Jana. She was older and had always been like a second mom to me. She was one of my favorite people in the whole world. But she worked full time, which meant that my grandmother (Jana's mom) would be with my baby during the day. Jana had four kids of her own, but they were all older, with her youngest being nine years old. Teen pregnancy and adoption were things she knew a lot about, and she'd already told me that she wanted me to play an active role in my baby's life.

Either choice would make a great home for my baby. I loved both families, and I knew they loved me and my baby. Either choice was a win-win situation. I decided to go back to the original list of the things I thought at the very beginning, the things that would be best for my baby. That way, I could get all the emotion out of the decision and try to make it logically.

I decided to go over to Bethany's house to visit with her and ask some detailed questions in an effort to get to know her better. I wanted to see her in her element, in her own home. I wanted to get a sense of what "normal" was like for her. Although she was my aunt, I'd never been very close to her. I knew I needed to get to know her better before making my choice. After spending some time talking with her, I knew it was time for us to meet with them.

Wrestling with the BIG Decision

Jeff and Bethany invited us to dinner one night so we could get to know each other better. Of course, it was a little awkward because we were all trying so hard to feel each other out. Jeff and Bethany had a few concerns they wanted to talk about with us. They wanted to be sure that, if at some point in the future Bryan and I ever got married, that we wouldn't try to get the baby back. We assured them that neither situation would happen. By the time we left, we all felt like it went well.

I knew I needed to make a decision soon, but I was concerned that Jeff and Bethany didn't understand how hard it was for me to make this decision. I was concerned that they didn't know much about the adoption process and couldn't appreciate how big of a sacrifice this was for me.

I tried to discuss the options with my parents, but they would always say, "You know what to do; you're smart. You hear God's voice." But all I could think was, *"I DO NOT HEAR GOD'S VOICE! HE IS SILENT! HE IS MAD! HE WON'T TALK TO ME!"*

I tried to pray, but it felt weird every time. I felt too much shame. I felt that I didn't deserve help from God or from anyone else. I needed to figure this out on my own. I got myself into this mess; I needed to get myself out of it.

Of course, I know now that this was a lie from the devil. God wanted to be closer to me than ever. God wanted to hold my broken heart, but I was so sad and so confused, I didn't know how to let Him comfort me. I continued to try to pray, but it was as if I had to relearn … completely rebuild my relationship with God. I didn't think I could even say the right words. I wanted to just ask God what to do and see His answer highlighted in my mind like words on a page. I wanted Him to just tell me what to do.

It had been so long since I felt like I'd heard God speak to me, I wasn't even confident that I would recognize His voice or know it when I heard it. I wanted it to be obvious. I wanted angels to sing and stars to streak through the sky or the earth to rumble.

It's like the story of the prophet Elijah waiting on the Lord to come. The Lord told him to stand on the mountain because He was going to pass by. While Elijah waited, a powerful wind came through and tore the mountain apart, but the Bible says, "The Lord was not in the wind." And after the wind was an earthquake, but God wasn't in the earthquake either. Nor was God in the fire that came next. But the Lord was in the "gentle whisper" that came after the fire (1 Kings 19:11-12).

We're tempted to have these grand illusions about what God is like or what it'll be like when He deals with us or speaks to us. In fact, God has a way of coming to us and speaking with us in a much different way than we're expecting Him to.

Those who were following Jesus were used to seeing Him heal the sick, lame, and blind. But they must have all been surprised to watch Him heal the blind man in the temple by spitting in the dirt, making mud, and rubbing it in the man's eyes (John 9:6-7). I think the Lord likes to catch us off guard.

And just like He did with Elijah, when it came time for me to make the decision about who should adopt my baby, God spoke to me so quietly, in a "gentle whisper." Whenever I would think about Jeff and Bethany as the adoptive parents, God would just gently calm my heart; He was so subtle not to scare me in my fragile state. He was directing me without having to send down an earthquake, a fire, or a huge revelation. By experiencing His calmness, I felt that God was telling me that Jeff and Bethany were the best option for my baby girl. I was certain I had heard from God. Now all I had to do was to trust Him.

A Difficult Conversation

Before I went to talk to Bethany about my decision, I knew I needed to talk to Jana. I'd spent time with Bethany and Jeff and we'd talked about the possibility of adoption, but I'd never discussed the possibility with Jana and I felt bad about it. She'd offered me a tremendous gift and showed me so much love, and I felt like I'd left her hanging. I just assumed from the beginning that I would meet with Jeff and Bethany first because I had so much more to learn about them. Then I was going to meet with Jana ... I already knew her so well. I just never expected to be so sure about my decision before talking with Jana.

My dad called Jana and asked if we could take her out for a cup of coffee. Because Jana is my dad's sister, I was grateful that he had offered to go with me to talk to her. The last thing in the world I wanted to do was to hurt my Aunt Jana. I would want her as my own mother if something ever happened to mine.

We sat down for coffee and made some small talk before I told her that I was choosing Bethany. I began to cry as the words came out, and of course, that made her cry too. I told her that it was what we thought was the best fit for the baby and it had nothing to do with her. It was heartbreaking. Jana would have made a great mom for my baby girl, but it was not God's will. She was so understanding. After our conversation was over, I felt like a huge weight had been lifted, the hard part was over. The path was clear now. The search for the best parents was OVER. I was so glad that I had made my choice.

Delivering the News

I wanted to tell Jeff and Bethany in a fun way that Bryan and I were giving them our baby. I thought of all kinds of creative ways but in the end, I decided on a cake because ... who doesn't love cake? I went to Walmart to place the order, but I wasn't sure what to put on it. It wasn't like I could write, *"Want to Adopt My Baby?"* or *"Hey, Have a Baby on Me!"*

I thought of when a baby girl is delivered they say to the parents, "IT'S A GIRL!" Even though Jeff and Bethany already knew it was a girl, I decided that's what I wanted on the cake. It's just the classic line that's said when you have a baby.

I talked to the lady behind the bakery counter and explained what I wanted it to say and asked if she knew of a cute way to decorate. She explained the trending idea of the cake frosting inside reflecting the sex of baby for gender reveals. Inwardly I rolled my eyes and thought, *"Oh boy, here we go again, I am going to have to explain to some stranger about adoption; they're going to give me a weird face, and pretend that they understand."*

So I went on to explain that I was telling a couple that they would be getting my daughter, I was choosing them to adopt my baby. But we all knew that the baby was a girl. So this wasn't a gender-reveal, it was a couple-reveal. The lady gave me a face I wasn't sure how to interpret. She said, "WOW, what a great idea! I love it! I was adopted too. My mom placed me in a closed adoption, and I have the most wonderful parents and have had the most wonderful life. Later on, I found my birth mother and she is amazing. We've become really close friends."

I could not believe this; it felt like another confirmation from the Lord that I was doing the right thing. God won't ask us to do something without confirming it to us over and over. It's like markers along the hiking trail that show you that you're on the right path. Without those markers you could easily wander off the trail so you continue to look for the signs along the way to confirm that you're heading in the right direction. God's "confirmation markers" can be anything from a scripture you read during a quiet time, to a feeling of peace that comes over you as you think about your situation, to a random conversation with a woman working the bakery counter at Walmart.

I asked her if everything worked out and if she cared that she was adopted. She said that she was so grateful that she was adopted and that she loved her life. I began to cry. I knew everything was going to be okay. Like this lady, there are people all around us who've been adopted and they made it just fine! They love their life, they love their adoptive parents, and they love their birth parents. I was so encouraged. That could be my story too!

The big day was June 7th. I had sent Bethany a text earlier and asked if Bryan and I could stop by to talk to her and Jeff. I was going to ask them to parent my baby girl. My first thought was, *what other teenager would be having such a monumental decision just three days before their 19th birthday?* This was the day that I would seal the decision that would chart the course of this child's whole life. This would affect what type of person this girl would become.

Bryan came and picked me up, and I sobbed the entire 15-minute car ride to their house. Then we had to sit in the car for another 20 minutes so I could get myself together. I kept thinking about all the things I was going to miss out on. My baby girl's whole life was playing out before my eyes, and I was not her mother in any of those scenes. The fact was, Bethany would be her mom and I would not. This baby girl that I loved so much would never call me "Mommy." I wanted to be her mom so bad, but I had to do what was best for her. I had to obey what God had asked me to do. Giving her to Jeff and Bethany was hard, but it was the best thing for her.

Being a good mom is always doing what's best for your child, and that's what I was doing. My willingness to give my baby to Jeff and Bethany Pepin showed that I was a good mom whether I had the title or not.

After calming down, we showed up at their front door. I am sure my red face and squinty, blotchy eyes shocked them. We went upstairs to their loft, and I made awkward small talk as I held the cake in my lap. Then I began to give my little spiel. "We would like to ask you to raise our baby…." That's all I could get out before starting to sob again. I remember looking at their fuzzy faces through my tears. I think I explained my hopes and dreams for the baby and shared how we thought they would be great parents. I may have even thrown something in about God. I hardly remember what I said. My words were all jumbled, and I am sure my sentences barely made sense through all my sobbing and trying to gather my thoughts.

I handed them the cake that had cute little pink booties. They were very happy and thanked us. We had quite a night—a night we'll remember forever.

We left shortly after and headed to Sonic to get ice cream. I had finally finished crying. Although my heart was completely broken, I felt relief. There was a plan in place now. I no longer had to worry about my baby's future home or what we were going to do. I was no longer overthinking the decision and felt a complete peace that I had made the right choice. Things were settled. Now I just had to make it through two more months of pregnancy … through the summer … with the record high temperature most days … of over 100 degrees.

CHAPTER 21

Scarlet

POLKA-DOT TOPS AND SHORTS

The past several days I had obsessed with the baby's future and whether or not I was hearing clearly from the Lord concerning my role in it. As I pushed my vacuum back and forth over the brown zebra-printed rug in our living room, I prayed and pleaded with God, "Are You sure, Lord? Am I really hearing You? Is Bethany the one to raise this baby girl? Please show me again, one more time. Please, Lord."

I felt a little like Gideon in the Bible (Judges 6). Even though Gideon was scared and in hiding, the Lord had visited him and told him that he was a "mighty warrior." God wanted Gideon to do mighty things for Him. But even after several confirmations, Gideon still wasn't sure it was God who was calling him.

So Gideon put out a fleece, or a sheepskin, on the ground, and said to God, "If there is dew only on the fleece and all the ground is dry, then I will know that you will save Israel by my hand, as you said" (Judges 6:37).

As crazy as that request was, God granted it. The next morning when Gideon went out to check on the fleece, it was just as he prayed. The ground was dry but the fleece was soaked. So much so that Gideon was able to squeeze a bowl full of dew out of it.

If you're like me, that would be plenty of confirmation! If I put a request like that before the Lord and He actually granted it, I would be positively sure that God was in what He had called me to do.

But it wasn't enough for Gideon. He had another prayer for the Lord. This time he started out by saying, "Do not be angry with me. Let me make just one more request." He went on, "Allow me one more test with the fleece, but this time make the fleece dry and let the ground be covered with dew" (Judges 6:39).

God answered that prayer too, just like Gideon requested. Finally Gideon was convinced and followed through on all God asked him to do. But what about us? What do we do when we *think* we know what God is calling us to, but we're not positive, we're just not sure?

Brennan Manning tells the story about a man struggling for direction so he went on a pilgrimage to pray and serve at the orphanage in India founded by Mother Teresa. After a few days their paths crossed, and Mother Teresa asked the man, "How can I pray for you?"

The man had a ready answer. He said, "I need direction. I'm not sure what to do with my life. I'm not sure where God is leading me. Will you pray that God will give me clarity?"

She answered him firmly but with kindness and love, "I will *not* pray for God to bring you clarity. Clarity is the last thing you are clinging to and must let go of. I have never had clarity; what I have always had is trust. So I will pray that you will trust God."[1]

Trusting God is one of the hardest things we must do as Christians. Learning to follow a God we cannot see is tough and requires us to use

---

[1] Brennan Manning, *Ruthless Trust, The Ragamuffin's Path to God,* New York, NY: HarperCollins, 2002, 5.

our faith. We love Him by faith. We serve Him by faith. And we believe that He leads us by faith. It was time for me to stop asking for "just one more confirmation" and muster my faith and trust that God was leading us where He wanted us to go.

The doorbell rang and I was hit with a wave of joy as I caught a glimpse through the front window of Bethany and little Reese, her 9 month old, on my porch. They had brought their swimsuits and were planning on jumping into the pool with Lindsay.

Bethany and Lindsay were slowly getting to know each other better as birth mom and adoptive mom instead of just niece and aunt. My relationship was changing with this pair as well. I was bonding more with Reese whom I no longer saw as my niece but now as my new granddaughter.

As usual, Bethany looked stunning and I'm not exaggerating. I have never seen Bethany not look absolutely beautiful. She was a pageant beauty and a former Miss Teen Louisiana. As I got to know her deeper with each encounter, I was delighted to find a friend with such spiritual depth. She was a kindred spirit of sorts who spoke the same language I did. It was no coincidence that during each of my pregnancies, Brad and I considered naming our baby "Bethany."

As I flung open the door, Bethany, with Reese on her hip, stepped out of the heat and into the coolness of the air conditioning. Both of them looked tan in their adorable summer outfits. Bethany had on a hot pink top with bright yellow polka-dots. As Lindsay came down the stairs to greet them, I was shocked to see that Lindsay was wearing a solid pink top, and her pink shorts were covered in the exact same bright yellow polka-dots that Bethany was wearing.

I smiled and felt a warm peace come over me as I realized that God was giving me the gift of yet another confirmation, revealing once again that

Bethany was to be our baby girl's new momma, and that these two young women were being knit together in Heaven.

You're probably thinking, *"You don't give a baby away just because an outfit matches!"* Yes, I know, I know. But like Gideon's fleece, this was just one more sign on top of a whole stack of signs that God was in the details and that we were on the right track.

Although I didn't know how the whole situation was going to work out, I did know that God knew. The deep sense of peace I was feeling could only have come from Him.

Lindsay—God Sends Comfort

As more and more people found out about the pregnancy, I was overwhelmed with the love of those surrounding me. I was flooded with so many kind words written in all my graduation and birthday cards. Several women texted me saying that they had had an unplanned pregnancy as well. I was blown away by all the love and acceptance I received. Tons of people were showing compassion and their willingness to help me out however they could. I was shocked at how many of my friends' parents gave me so much love. They could have seen me as a negative influence or a bad kid. But instead, I was welcomed into their homes, fed plenty of snacks, and even given a children's book for my baby.

When it came to my part-time job as a babysitter, I was really nervous. I wasn't sure how to tell the parents what was going on with me. I didn't want them to think I was a bad role model. But in the end, there was nothing to worry about. I couldn't believe how many people showed me love, acceptance, and understanding. I was always nervous when I had to tell a family about my pregnancy. I will never forget the families that would say, "Oh, no problem at all; we'll be sure to use you even more. We want to help you out in your time of need."

I even had one lady give me my very first "Congratulations!" It was nice to not be judged, but covered in love. The ladies from CPO were helping me get more job opportunities by giving out my number to moms who visited the CPO support groups. I was amazed. The kids I sat for never seemed to mind either. They barely noticed … or even cared.

I had one five year old ask me, "Is there a baby in your tummy?" I replied, "Yes." She just said, "Okay" and continued to watch her show on television. It made me laugh how, at the end of the day, everyone just looked at me and thought, *Okay, she's pregnant, so what?* Although not every family was okay with me watching their children, I had more than enough jobs to keep gas in my car.

The kindness shocked me as it continued to pour in. One of the biggest gifts of love I received was from my Aunt Jana. She threw a baby shower for Bethany and me. I remember she showed me compassion, even celebrating a baby that at one point she thought might be hers. People brought baby items for Bethany and fun personal items for me. I was showered in massage gift cards, pedicure gift cards, and greeting cards filled with the kindest words. I couldn't believe everyone was this generous, making me feel loved and celebrated.

When things get tough, it's crazy how God sends people to comfort you and help you. I couldn't have made it through without everyone's kindness. The true sign of a Christian is when they go overboard to love someone, even someone who is hurting because of their own sin. I was surrounded by people who chose grace over judgment, support over neglect, and love over indifference. That sounds like Jesus to me.

My Baby Gets a Name

We finally had the adoptive parents picked out, so naturally now we wanted to know what her name would be. All throughout the pregnancy

I carefully guarded myself from the temptation to name my baby. I knew naming her would make me feel like she was mine, ultimately making it harder to give her up. I also didn't want to give my baby a name when rightfully Bethany should be the one to name her.

So since the baby didn't have a name yet, my family settled on calling her "baby girl." I usually just referred to her as my "little friend." As I started to accept that she was inside me, I viewed her as my friend who came along with me on all my adventures. As soon as I told Bethany that she would be getting my baby, I wanted to know if she had thought about any names. My mom and I asked her several different times about names. She always said she had some ideas but she never told us what they were. I didn't want to pressure her … but I was dying to know!

One day Bethany and I were picking out items for the baby registry, and she told me that she had selected a name but wanted to make sure I liked it. I was instantly filled with excitement, but I was also nervous as we stood there in the store, across the rack filled with baby items. I was just telling myself, *"Even if you don't like it, smile!"* I was hoping for the best, but preparing for the worst.

But when she said the name, I didn't have to fake my smile. I instantly fell in love with it. She had chosen the name "Kinley." She went on to tell me that the reason she liked it was because it meant "Warrior" and "Defender." She had a Bible verse that went with it as well. "Defend the weak and the fatherless; uphold the cause of the poor and the oppressed. Rescue the weak and the needy; deliver them from the hand of the wicked" (Psalm 82:3-4). I was so happy that I finally got to hear the name and that my baby was no longer going to be referred to as just "the baby" or "baby girl." She was Kinley! The beautiful baby in my belly had a name!

And not just any name, but a powerful and strong name! This was just another reminder to me that every baby is born for a purpose and that God has a plan for every child whether the pregnancy was planned or not.

In the Bible, a person's name was often aligned with their purpose or their character. There are even instances where God Himself actually gives someone a new name, a name that fits their calling much better than the name they were given at birth. Just think, Abraham, Sarah, Israel, Peter, Paul, and many more ... were all names given to people by God and not by their birth parents.

At this point, I wasn't sure what God's plan for Kinley was going to be, but I felt exactly right about the name Bethany had chosen. With a name that means "Warrior" and "Defender," I knew she would be destined for great things.

While at lunch together, Bethany and I discussed middle names. She said that she wanted a one-syllable name, and she mentioned using her middle name, which is May. I thought that was a great idea because then it would make Kinley feel special and accepted into her new family. But secretly I wanted her to have my middle name, Joy (which is one syllable as well!). I wanted to feel like I was Kinley's parent too, but just like the first name, the middle name wasn't up to me. I wasn't going to be Kinley's mother.

A couple of weeks had gone by, and I just assumed that Kinley's middle name was going to be May. Bethany called me late one night and said that she talked with Jeff about it, and they both felt like God was telling them to have Kinley's middle name be Joy! I was so excited that I started to cry. Not that crying wasn't already a constant thing with me anyway! Her gesture meant so much to me.

The fact that they picked Joy was very special to me, just like a hug and a gift from God. I didn't want to tell anyone right away except for my family. I wanted to savor this special moment and not share it with the world. I waited a long time to tell my friends because I just wanted to hold it close and keep it to myself.

Finally, I had a fun secret to keep! This was something special, just between my baby and me. I was filled with so much happiness. Things were falling into place, and the fact that my middle name had been chosen for Kinley proved that I still had a place in this plan. God was so faithful that, in what seemed like a hopeless situation, He brought hope. He was the One who brought the JOY!

CHAPTER 22

Scarlet

PURPLE CRAYON

n a few weeks I would have to watch my precious little girl give birth to her daughter, and then place her precious little girl in another mother's arms to forever hold and take as her own. I knew deep in my gut and spirit that this was God's plan. He had confirmed to me over and over again that Jeff and Bethany were to be Kinley's parents. I knew that this was what He was telling me as sure as I knew anything He'd ever spoken to my heart before.

I continued to remind myself of this, and yet my emotions were rebelling. Deep within the layers of my being, the swarming questions made me feel like a scared little two-year-old girl. What would the delivery be like? How would Lindsay be able to do this? What was my role to be? Was Lindsay a woman or was she still a child? Was it okay to continue to "mother" her, or would that only keep her from being able to make the grown-up decision she was facing?

I pondered these thoughts and continued to ask my Lord to give me strength and even more insight, and that's exactly what He did. As I sat on my couch journaling early one August morning, trying to sip my coffee, made difficult because of the lump in my throat, God reminded me of something I hadn't thought about in years.

As I prayed, He guided my thoughts back to a memory of an incident that took place during spring break of my freshman year of college. A friend, Carl Krane, and I were driving from Tulsa home to Orlando to visit our families. When I realized there would be only two drivers on this long trip, I made a plan that if one of us was driving, the other would be sleeping, resting up for our future driving duties. All things considered, it would be worth the trip to have a week of vacation at home and hopefully some beach time.

About halfway through the journey, as I slept in the backseat, I was jarred into a sudden panic as I felt our car make a 360-degree spin on the four-lane highway going 55 miles per hour.

Seconds later, Carl was able to pull the car over to the side of the road, and we got out without a scratch on us. Thank God we were okay, but as I looked down the steep embankment, I was shocked to see another car deep in the ditch. My heart was racing and my hands were sweating as I made my way down the steep slope about 50 yards still trying to figure out exactly what had happened.

There on the grass ahead of me sat a little girl just staring straight ahead. She looked to be about five years old, and her face was completely absent of any expression. I slowly sat down next to her as she grasped a purple crayon tightly in her little palm. I assumed that she had been coloring in her car just moments before.

The crayon represented the last shred of "normal" she was to know before being flung into a whole new world; a world of sitting on the side of a highway in the grass while a black-headed college girl tried to assure her that she was going to be okay.

Oh, baby girl. She looked so frail and small as she held on tightly to her crayon. Maybe she didn't even know it was still in her hand. It was the day, she would later learn, that her grandmother crossed the center line on the highway, lost control, and was thrown out of the car to her death. I sat with this tiny child for at least 30 minutes while Carl searched the over-grown brush down the embankment and found her grandmother's body. Later, he reported to us that the paramedics were working to try to revive her as they performed CPR. The little girl never said a word.

The Memory's Meaning

As the Lord brought me back to this scene in my memory, I realized that He was giving me some direction, some meaning to go with that incident that had happened so many years before. He revealed to me that now I was the little girl, shocked and stunned as I watched this very unexpected, life-changing scene play out before my eyes.

Just a short eight months before, I was simply coloring with my purple crayon, living a "normal" life, raising three daughters, sitting in the car and riding along the road of life. It was as if He was highlighting that purple crayon. He was comforting me and validating the human emotions I was having.

He was letting me know that I was in a new scene in my life, one that I never saw coming. He was telling my heart that it was okay for me to tightly grasp in my sweaty palm the crayon from my last "normal."

In my case, the crayon was my daughter; the normal purple crayon represented the mothering of my second daughter, Lindsay Joy Pepin. He was impressing upon me that it was okay for me to feel these nurturing, motherly feelings towards her; they were normal. Essentially He was letting me know that I would continue to be there to hold her and to love her and to nurture my little girl as she released her little girl into a new family.

I knew that Lindsay was a grown woman. I understood that she had made an adult decision to have sex and that by choosing adoption she was making the most adult decision of her life. She was making the decision to choose what was best for her daughter, even though everything in her natural flesh wanted to hold on to her.

I knew that it would take intense courage, and I respected Lindsay immensely for making this sacrificial choice. Woman to woman, mother to mother, I now saw Lindsay, in some ways, as an equal. I knew that I would never have to make this monumental decision myself, but now my role was to help this fellow mother, whom I greatly respected, in any way that I could. I would be in the delivery room with her, buy her flowers, and make her meals. Whatever it took. Yes, I would mother this new young, brave mother.

God was letting me know that it was okay for me to hold on to my purple crayon.

CHAPTER 23

Scarlet

CAN I BE MIMI?

"What will the baby call us?" I asked Jeff and Bethany as they sat on our family room couch while Reese crawled around on the zebra print rug.

"Whatever names you and Brad want to be called. We just want all of our children to call you guys the same thing."

I answered very quickly, "I would love to be Mimi, but Brad isn't sure what grandpa name he wants yet." I was thrilled to know that Bethany was okay with us having grandparents' names because Kinley would be raised in our huge extended family, and I was hoping that I wouldn't just be labeled "Scarlet" or worse, "Aunt Scarlet."

I never wanted her to think that I was her aunt. Instead, I wanted her to know that I was her biological maternal grandmother. I wanted to be there during every stage of her life, cheering her on, explaining any questions she was bound to have about her birth and adoption. But most of all, I wanted her to know how much I loved her and how much I would always love her.

"Bethany, do you think your parents will be okay with us having grandparent names?" I was well aware that once Lindsay and Bryan released legal rights as Kinley's birth mother and father that Jeff and Bethany would legally be her parents and therefore her adoptive grandparents would always hold the "top grandparent" spot. I wanted to know how Bethany's parents were feeling; I took Bethany's report of her mother's reaction to Kinley becoming her new granddaughter seriously. Her mother had told Bethany, "I will love the baby just as much as if she was my own."

I, in turn, opened up my heart wide to Jeff and Bethany's daughter Reese and any other children they would have. I wanted them to know how loved they all were. There is no way that a child can be surrounded by too much love. To this day when Brad and I babysit Reese and Kinley, they enjoy seeing both of their toddler pictures on Mimi and Pops' wall. Oh yeah, Brad picked "Pops" as his name.

Lindsay—Getting Back with the Lord

As the summer went on, I worked hard to prepare my heart for not only having this baby but also for giving her up for adoption. But I was also trying hard to get my life back on track with the Lord because I knew I wouldn't be able to go through the pain of placing my baby up for adoption without Him. I went to church regularly, and one particular Sunday I accepted the call to come down front to the altar. That's where I recommitted my life to the Lord.

It felt weird. I had tons of spiritual "head knowledge." I'd been a Christian for over 15 years, but I was just so damaged. I didn't want my Heavenly Father to see me in the midst of my pain. I believed the lie that I had to fix myself, or "get right" before coming to the Lord. I thought that unless I was righteous that God wouldn't accept me. I knew He loved me, but I was ashamed to let Him close to me. Consequently, I was working hard to get my life back on track but feeling like I was failing miserably.

I would hear stories about people who would be so broken that they would fully surrender to the Lord on the spot and somehow immediately be "all better." It was hard for me to fully surrender to Him, because my pride and shame wouldn't allow me. My sin and brokenness caused me to have such an awkward relationship with the Lord. I kept feeling His presence, I always knew He was right there next to me but, in hindsight, I can see that I was the one who didn't want to get too close to Him. In my view, getting close meant that I would be exposed, revealing all of my nasty sin.

As I continued my journey of learning how to pray again, it became something that I had to talk to Him about out loud. I just talked to Him like He was in the room with me. Often, my "talking" would turn into sobbing, even yelling. My heart was getting ripped out and God wasn't fixing it. This level of pain was something I had never experienced before, emotional pain that was so deep I could feel it physically. I was literally groaning, pleading with God to fix it.

I would yell at Him through my tears, "I WILL OBEY! I WILL GIVE HER UP! PLEASE JUST DON'T MAKE IT HURT ANYMORE! PLEASE TAKE AWAY THE PAIN! PLEASE! I BEG YOU! I WILL BE GOOD … JUST MAKE IT STOP!" I had made the right decision to give up my baby, and everyone told me how brave I was and that they were so proud of me. But if I was doing the right thing, why didn't I feel better? Why did I still hurt almost all the time?

You can probably recognize by that kind of language that this was the "bargaining stage" of my grief. I didn't understand why He didn't just make the pain go away. I didn't understand that this pain was not only helping me learn to trust Christ again, but it was also building up my warrior heart. I would sob like this often and plead with God to stop the pain. But I never felt the pain let up. Not once did I feel even one ounce of relief.

I have since learned that pain can sometimes be a good thing. Like a child who burns their hand on a hot stove … learning valuable lessons can be painful. But pain teaches us. Pain helps us grow into resilient people who are dependent on Christ.

Hebrews 12:11 says, "No discipline seems pleasant at the time, but painful. Later on, however, it produces a harvest of righteousness and peace for those who have been trained by it." It's not odd for "the right thing" to be the painful thing. Working out or dieting isn't always fun and can even be painful. But the ones who are able to stick with it will find themselves healthier and stronger in the end.

The truth is, obedience hurts and it's not always easy. I wonder if Abraham from the Bible felt the same pain I did as he obeyed the Lord and brought his son Isaac to the altar to be sacrificed. I wonder if Abraham begged God to take away the pain of that obedient decision like I did.

Looking back now, I wouldn't trade that pain for anything else in the world. The pain I felt during those months resulted in my beautiful daughter. And it was that pain that shaped me into the strong woman I am today. I now know I can do tough things. It was His discipline that built a warrior's heart in me.

Finding the Words in Worship

As the begging with God continued, I went to church one Sunday and the worship team started to sing. From the very first line of the song, it was like the songwriter had written the song just for me.

As I read and sang the words up on the screen, I realized that they were the exact words I'd been trying to pray for months. We sang about healing and about cleansing, about calling out to God for peace and freedom.

There was even a line about placing your life in His arms. Those were my feelings exactly.

After singing those lyrics I felt like it was time to surrender my precious baby to Him, no conditions, no hesitations. I felt like for the first time I could trust God with my baby. I was done trying to bargain with God. I was ready to give my baby to the Lord, no strings attached.

As I continued to worship, I imagined myself laying my baby at the foot of the cross. I told Him, "I place my baby in Your strong arms. Please bring peace to my soul." I heard Him say back to my heart as clear as day, "I understand. You know, I had to give up My baby too."

WOW! The floodgates blew open, and I could not stop crying. I had never thought of that before. This God who I had felt so awkward around up until that day had gone through exactly the same thing I was going through. He was so close to me the whole time. The God of the universe completely understood my pain. He had walked where I was currently walking.

Hebrews 4:15 says, "For we do not have a high priest who is unable to empathize with our weaknesses, but we have one who has been tempted in every way, just as we are—yet he did not sin." Because God came to earth in the form of a man, Jesus, He is very well acquainted with our weaknesses. He knows the kinds of things that tempt us, baffle us, give us joy … or give us pain. Because of this, His compassion is complete. He is able to comfort us like a friend who knows *exactly* what we're going through … because He's been there before.

I felt like I was finally connecting with God because we were both parents. Not only were we both parents, but we were both parents of a child who was being raised by someone else. We were both parents who had to give up their babies.

Now I knew that God was the first one to ever fully understand my heart. I had never sensed so much comfort. All the times that I felt like people just didn't get it, He got it all along. He understood my pain. I had surrendered for the first time, and He immediately swooped in and picked me up. For the first time in the last seven months, my broken heart was beginning to beat again. For the first time ever, I could understand and identify with Psalm 147:3, which says, "He heals the brokenhearted and binds up their wounds." That's exactly what God was doing in me. He was healing my broken heart ... binding up my deep wounds. He was demonstrating His unconditional love for me by holding me close, even though I might cry and yell, argue and rant. God loved me and would not leave my side, no matter how ugly I might get.

A Confirming Conversation

It was getting closer and closer to my due date and Reese, Bethany's daughter, had a birthday coming up. My mom and I decided to get "Big Sister" and "Little Sister" onesies made for the two girls.

When I arrived at the embroidery shop I told the lady what I wanted to have monogrammed. I knew she could tell I was pregnant; it was pretty obvious by this time. She looked at me and asked if I already had another baby. I am sure she was shocked that a girl my age would have a little girl old enough to be a "big sister" at home. I remember instantly thinking, *"Oh no. Here we go again!"*

I didn't want to have to lie or try to change the subject so I decided to just explain the whole situation to this woman I didn't even know. By now, I was getting really good at it. I launched off into the story I normally tell and even while the words were coming out of my mouth, I had the feeling I was being judged.

She looked back at me with the funniest expression as we stood facing each other in the tiny tee-shirt shop. I thought, *Oh, crap. She doesn't get it or she thinks I'm horrible for giving up my baby.* I just got the story out as quickly as I could and braced myself for her response.

She smiled and replied with a simple, "Oh." Then she paused, looked at me and said, "Do you mind me asking how old you are?" I told her that I was 19, thinking that she was judging me. I thought she was probably a strict religious woman ready to say, "Bless your heart" in a condescending, judgmental way. I quickly explained my reasons for the adoption, once again feeling like I had to justify myself to not get judged. I couldn't believe I was sitting there explaining a nine-month thought process to a complete stranger.

She finally said that her twin daughters were adopted, and her sister had adopted kids too. Instantly I felt a wave of relief wash over me. Instead of thinking I was about to go on the chopping block, I was completely surprised. She told me how proud of me she was and how she thought I was doing the right thing. She followed that up with some strong advice to keep my heart open and keep the adoption open because her daughters wish they knew their birth parents like her sister's kids did.

This was one more confirmation that I was doing the right thing. The conversation with that woman gave me the reassurance that Kinley would grow up just fine and that she would have a successful life. I was holding on to so much fear about the future of this little baby, but these days of reassuring encounters helped me let go of the fear and provided me with the peace and confidence to keep going.

CHAPTER 24

Scarlet

THE COUNSELOR WANTS TO SEE ME

t was Tuesday afternoon, just two weeks before Lindsay's due date, and my mind was occupied, wondering what Lindsay had been discussing in the last hour with her counselor. As I wiped down the kitchen counters for what seemed like the hundredth time, I heard the front door close, and I watched Lindsay waddle in to the house belly first. Her long, brown suntanned legs and thin, firm arms screamed "high schooler," but her pregnant belly protruding out in front of her screamed "adult."

Lindsay was now in the place of having to walk out a full-blown, adult, life-altering decision. She was only two weeks away from forever changing her child's life … as well as her own. Like every week after her counseling session, I wanted to grab her by the shoulders and look deep into her eyes to see how she was doing. Actually, it wasn't just on counseling days that I wanted to do this; it was every day, several times a day. I wanted to force her to look at me and ask her a hundred times over, "What's on your heart? Are you sure about choosing adoption?"

I kept wiping the same counters that I felt I had been wiping for the last 21 years. It seemed that as soon as I got married, I was handed a wash rag and was given 21 years of counter duty, 21 years of mothering, mothering and laundry, mothering and carpooling, mothering and sweeping. But in all my years of mothering and future mothering, I would have never predicted that I would be wiping those counters while wanting to pull out all of my teenager's thoughts and feelings concerning her pregnancy and adoption plan.

"So how are you?" I asked as nonchalantly as possible.

"She wants to meet with you."

"The counselor?"

"Yeah, she wants to talk to you."

Oh, shoot! My thoughts raced. *I must be doing something wrong. Lindsay probably told her stuff about me. Oh, crap. No. Wait a minute. I actually want to meet with the counselor. I want her to know my side of the story. In fact, I have tons to say and maybe, if I'm lucky, she'll tell me a little bit about what Lindsay is thinking.*

While my mind was whirling in thought, Lindsay continued, "You're supposed to call her."

"Okay, no problem. Any other news?"

"Nope, I don't want to talk about it."

"Okay," I whispered. I put my head back down and tried to focus on the spot I'd been wiping since Lindsay came into the room.

New Information

A week later I was pulling my car into the CPO parking lot feeling more than just a little apprehensive. I knew that the counselor would be open-minded, having sat across from many different kinds of families, but

I couldn't help feeling like I was wearing a sticker on my shirt that said, "HELLO! My Name is Mother of Pregnant High Schooler."

When I entered her office, I saw a couch facing a single chair where she sat with a manila folder labeled "PEPIN." I assumed it held papers containing notes of all of her observations.

I found myself in that moment being immensely grateful to this organization that offered free Christian counseling to unwed mothers. Not only was counseling offered to the birth mother during the pregnancy but for the remainder of her life. This wise counselor had even offered to meet with our 14-year-old, Gabrielle, to talk about how she was handling her family's situation.

As I looked at the big clock up on the wall, I wondered what it might be like to be her. When the clock signaled the end of her day, she had the luxury of being able to simply close up her file of notes, lock up her office, and go home to have dinner with her family.

But it wasn't that easy for me. I couldn't avoid the situation by simply closing a file and walking away. I wondered to myself if I had become obsessed with Lindsay's life.

She motioned for me to sit down on the couch and began our session by saying, "Thank you for coming and meeting with me."

Throughout the next hour we talked about things that only her years of experience in meeting families like ours could bring. She took my mind to places that it had never been before as she unfolded facts that were brand-new to me. She told me that oftentimes girls who place their babies for adoption will get pregnant soon afterwards in an effort to replace the missing piece in their grieving hearts. Her suggestion was that we should get Lindsay on birth control after the baby was born.

She explained that research had shown that when a teenager starts out raising her baby, by the age of two, the child is usually left in the grandparents' care as the new mother begins to date and the novelty of parenting has worn off.

Mother-to-mother she empathized with me. After talking with her for a bit, her deep understanding made me truly believe her words when she admitted to me, "I don't know what decision I would make if it was my child."

She explained the reason that she wanted to see me alone was that she wanted to make sure that I had taken the time to think this decision through … all the way through. She was checking to see if I was absolutely sure that I was not to raise or even help to raise Lindsay's baby. She said that in recent weeks she had seen situations at CPO where the birth mother had chosen to place her baby for adoption only to have the maternal grandmother interfere once she saw the infant. The grandmother convinced the newly postpartum birth mom that she shouldn't give her baby up. This story hit pretty close to home … I was the maternal grandmother.

The counselor looked at me seriously and encouraged me to figure out whether or not I was sure about supporting Lindsay's plan. She told me that if I wasn't in complete agreement with the decision, then I needed to voice that concern before the baby arrived.

She went on to explain the devastation and confusion that a maternal grandmother can cause for the adoptive family and for her own daughter. If the decision has been made that adoption is the best option for the child, then emotions, which can be fickle and unreliable, should not be allowed to override the decision at the last minute in the delivery room. I was once again reminded that as much as I might want to extract myself from the situation and just be a support for Lindsay, my guidance and voice did carry some weight. My opinion was going to play an important role in my beloved granddaughter's destiny.

What a weighty decision this was ... a decision I'd not signed up for. I had struggled to keep some distance, not becoming codependent, making my life all about Lindsay's life. But now a professional counselor was confirming the truth that my heart, my voice, and my convictions could change many lives ... forever.

As much as this role caught me by surprise eight months earlier, I now felt myself growing into my unique and influential role. As much as I had often wanted to simply run away from this responsibility, now I knew I could and would, with God's help, stay true to what God was leading me to do.

Lindsay—The Time Was Coming Soon

I knew that the baby's delivery was going to have to be by my due date because I had to start college just a week later. We had scheduled my induction weeks before, and I had one more appointment on Friday, August 10th, before being induced on Monday, the 13th.

The plan was for me to start community college the very next week, on the 20th of August, so the scheduling was pretty tight leading up to that week. My baby was going to be born in just a few days! All this was going through my mind in the middle of the night while my sister Alyssa was asleep in the bed next to mine. As usual, she was sleeping like a rock while I was tossing and turning, too hot and too uncomfortable to sleep.

But it was that night, lying in my bed, I finally accepted the reality of my pregnancy and giving my baby away. I completely accepted whatever was going to happen, and I stopped speculating on all the "what ifs." I released my control of the situation entirely. As I lay in the darkness and quietly talked to my baby, I told her that I loved her more than anything in the world. I did my best to explain the situation to her and why I was doing what I was doing. I told her we would both be okay. In that moment, I felt like Kinley and I truly had made a connection, that we had an understanding of what was going on and what was going to happen.

As the hot tears streamed down my face, I leaned in and prayed to God like I had never prayed before. I was up all night talking to my baby, talking to my Heavenly Father, and allowing His peace to rule and reign in my heart. I gave Him complete control and turned over my weak and broken heart for Him to carry in His big, strong arms. I knew I was going to be okay. I could do this. It was the first time in the last 40 weeks that I felt the pressure ease. I had made peace with my baby, peace with the situation, and peace with God, all in the dark of the night lying in my bed.

The following Thursday night, August 9th, I was over at a friend's house. A group of us were all hanging around before everyone left for college. We laughed and enjoyed each other. I was on my friend's bed, feeling big and pregnant, sitting "crisscross," hunched over my enormous belly. I felt the baby kick really hard under my ribs. Then about four minutes later she kicked again. This continued to happen several more times at regular intervals.

It was clear that something was going on. I was uncomfortable to be sure, but I'd been uncomfortable before in this pregnancy. No, I could tell, this was something different. Despite my feelings, I muddled through and did the best I could to enjoy the rest of the night just being a kid. I laughed and cried with my friends, knowing that we were all going on to our next chapter. They were going to college and joining a sorority while I would be going to a delivery room and enduring hard labor.

The next day, Friday the 10th, I went to my last OBGYN appointment. I was barely one centimeter dilated. As the doctor wrapped up the appointment, my mother and I confirmed that we would be good to go for induction on that coming Monday. The doctor gave us a surprised look and said she needed to go to her office for a moment to double-check her calendar and that she would be right back. When she returned she informed us that there had been a mix-up. She had accidentally double-booked that day and that I would not be able to be induced that Monday as we'd planned.

The doctor gave us two options: We could wait another week and induce on the next Monday the 20th, yes ... my first day of school, or I could get induced ... TODAY!

CHAPTER 25

Lindsay
TODAY!

Yes, when the doctor said, "Today," she meant the day that we were sitting in her office! Making the decision wasn't actually that hard. I knew I didn't want to wait until the following week because that's when my college classes were starting. As weird as it seemed, I would be starting school the very next week! So, it looked like this was going to have to be the day.

But it also meant I had no bags packed and was nowhere near ready mentally to have a baby. I did a quick check of my watch and saw that it was already 2:00. They wanted us to be checked into the hospital by 4:00 so I could be induced. I quickly did the math in my head. We lived 30 minutes from the hospital so that meant we had an hour-long trip home and back, which would give us just an hour at home to pull everything together.

The minute we got in the car, my mom and I got on our phones and started calling everyone to tell them the new schedule. The first person I called was Bethany. I told her about the change in plans, and we realized at the same time that Bethany's daughter Reese was going to be having her first birthday party on Saturday, which was the next day, so the party would have to be rescheduled. Bethany stayed calm and just kept repeating the words, "Okay. Okay." As she hung up, she was already thinking about her next step. She said, almost to herself, "I need to call Mom." Bethany's parents were planning on coming to town from Louisiana for the birth so they needed to know immediately about the change in plans.

Meanwhile, my mom called my dad and told him while I called Bryan, who had already left for college. I told him he needed to hurry, knowing he was an eight-hour drive away. Just to make sure, I also called his mother. They decided, based on the flights they were checking, that driving would actually get him back to Tulsa quicker than flying.

Of course, since I had been in so much denial about the baby, I had nothing packed to take to the hospital so I threw a few things in a bag; then I quickly showered and straightened my hair. I wanted to look good for all the pictures I knew would be taken! My heart was racing and my hands were shaking so much I could barely get my nails painted. But I wasn't going to have this baby without painted nails … bright red!

As I thought about what was ahead, I felt secure because there was finally a plan. I was going to the hospital, and they were going to induce my labor. For once I knew exactly how it was going to go and what to expect. There had been enough surprises over the last 40 weeks! We made it to the hospital by 4:00, and they immediately set me up in a room where they started to monitor both the baby and me.

What I didn't realize was that early labor had already begun. Once I got hooked up I could clearly see the contractions taking place, even though I couldn't feel them yet. Seeing the contractions on the monitor meant I didn't have to wonder whether or not I was in labor. I knew because the monitor told me I was! I was glad we were already in the hospital, in a controlled environment surrounded by people who knew what was going on and exactly how to take care of me. I needed that reassurance with all the crazy emotions that were to come.

As it turned out, they decided to wait to give me the Pitocin until the next morning. Pitocin is a drug that puts you into labor. At around 5:00 p.m., I no longer needed the monitor to tell me I was in labor. I could feel the contractions now, nothing big, but I knew something was happening.

Right around 6:30 I received my first visitor, my dad. He came in with a Subway sandwich, purple flowers, and a gift from my parents. It was a beautiful necklace that was a circle with an "L" on the front. But on the back was engraved, "Kinley Joy." This meant that Kinley would always be near to my heart, but they'd had the name engraved on the back of the necklace. That way I wouldn't have to deal with all the questions about what that name on my necklace meant. It was so thoughtful of my parents, and I really felt their support and love.

The three of us were now at the finish line. Through all the drama and tears, we stood there together, still a family, still loving and supporting each other. We'd been through a battle together, but we were still the Pepins—with a new one about join the family.

Shortly after my dad arrived, my doula showed up. Marlita was a woman we knew through our previous church; then we reconnected with her through CPO. Lots of women use doulas to help them through their labor and birth. Marlita was there to help provide emotional and physical support. I felt like she was my "insider," able to tell us what to expect, what the results of my tests meant, and how to deal with certain things. It was nice to have someone who wasn't emotionally involved available to help us navigate through the confusing process.

It wasn't long before Jeff and Bethany arrived with Reese. They came by to say hi and drop off a bunch of my favorite snacks plus another amazing gift. They gave me a ring that had Kinley's birthstone on it. They had also engraved the inside of the ring with her name. Since that night in the hospital, the ring has never left my finger.

Ever since Kinley was born, I've loved my necklace and my ring. They are both powerful symbols that remind me every day not only of how much I love Kinley, but also how much God loves me. They also represent the work God did in me through those months of my pregnancy.

Of course, there's another symbol that reminds us all of God's love for us … the cross of Christ. His love was strong enough to send His own Son to die in order to save us from sin and experience eternal life. Because of what Christ did on the cross, our sins were forgiven and we were reconciled back to God. The nail scars in the hands and feet of Jesus provide another powerful symbol of what God did on our behalf.

Because of the cross, we were reconciled with God. "Reconcile" means to restore relations or coexist in harmony. Our sin caused a division between God and us. But it was the cross of Christ that bridged that gap and brought us back together. My sin no longer separates me from God or His love … and yours doesn't separate you either. I think of that love every time I look in the mirror and see my necklace or look at my hand and notice my ring.

Now the visitors seemed to be coming in waves. After Jeff and Bethany left, my sisters arrived. It was around 8:00 p.m. and I had just eaten a red popsicle. That's when I really started to feel the pressure of having this baby, and the pressure caused me to feel edgy and out of sorts. So around 8:30 everyone left the room so I could have some space and rest for a bit before the serious labor kicked in. I lay in bed doing my best to get comfortable while my mom stayed with me in the room, sitting on the couch.

I was so blessed to have her by my side. We talked and ate snacks. Then the next wave of visitors appeared as Bryan arrived around 10:00. The lights in the room had already been turned out, but we were able to talk for a little bit. After a while, he left to go home and get some rest before the big day. At about 10:30 I was given some medicine to help me deal with the increasing pain and to help me get some sleep.

I awoke in a panic just a couple hours later. Hard labor was starting to kick in, and I found myself in some serious pain. But the pain wasn't just the physical pain coming from the contractions. I was also feeling the emotional effects of birthing a baby that would never be mine. My emotions were going crazy, no doubt made worse because of the medication I was on. But my mom was right there by my side holding me close and helping me catch my breath.

Looking back at that moment in my mind all I can see are dark, blurry images coming in and out of the room. I remember my labor intensifying, my baby coming soon. I'm in my bed, my body rocking back and forth. I'm crying to my mom, "ITS GOING TO HURT!" She asks me, "What's going to hurt? Giving birth or giving her up?" Through painful sobs I reply, "BOTH"!

Trust and Obey

I was on a collision course with these two new realities, giving birth and giving my baby up. And the contractions, now coming every two minutes, were a constant reminder. I was having this baby and I was giving her up, which meant that I was going to have to be more obedient than I had ever been in my life. I was going to have to fully trust that I heard the Lord about placing Kinley up for adoption with Bethany and Jeff. I was going to make the biggest sacrifice of my life and give away my most precious possession.

For about 90 minutes, I just rocked in the bed as my mom held me. She tried to help me focus through the contractions, but I was so hysterical just imagining what it was going to be like when they took my baby from my arms and gave her to Jeff and Bethany. There's no way I could have made it through those hours without my mom. She was holding her baby as I was crying about mine. It was a true expression of a mother's love shining through both of us.

Around 2:00 in the morning, my mom convinced me to get an epidural. I had known all along that I might need the help of the epidural, but I wanted to delay it as long as possible so I could experience the pain of giving birth. Somehow, I felt like I needed the physical pain so I'd always remember the birth of my first baby. But there was no way I could deal with the pain anymore. I was given the epidural around 2:30 in the morning.

Once the epidural kicked in, it was heaven. I couldn't feel a thing and was finally able to go back to sleep. And with the epidural to block the constant pain, I slept hard. At 5:00 a.m. my eyes opened and I was immediately wide awake. I'd slept so deeply, it felt like I had been asleep for a year. But now that I was awake, I grabbed my phone and looked at Facebook and let my mom continue to sleep.

All Ready for Kinley Joy

Around 5:25 in the morning I called the nurse to have her flip me to my other side. Because of my epidural I couldn't move by myself and needed her to help me change positions. She asked if I wanted her to check my dilatation. She had just checked about an hour and a half before so I was a little hesitant but had her check anyway. I'm glad I had her check … in that short time my dilation had doubled.

It's amazing how the body communicates whether you're awake or not. My body knew it was time for me to wake up even though I was completely out of it. My body knew it was time to wake up and have this baby. Within 30 minutes I was fully dilated and ready to deliver. We quickly called everyone to say "THE BABY IS ON THE WAY!"

The doctor on call came into the room and ruptured my water, then called my doctor to tell her that Kinley was coming quickly now. Shortly after that, it turned into a mad dash with everyone rushing into my room! First Bryan came in at 6:15; next came Marlita, the doula; then Bethany made it. After the rush of activity a sense of calm washed over the room. We were all in our places and all we were waiting for was the doctor … and Kinley!

CHAPTER 26

Scarlet

IT'S NOT ABOUT ME

We got Lindsay dressed in a flowy cotton backless hospital gown and settled her in to give birth to her daughter. Try as I might, I couldn't help personalizing this experience. I knew it wasn't all about me, but after all, my grandmother name was going to be "Mimi," pronounced, "Me Me"!

Sadly, it's human nature for us to put ourselves at the center of things and make every situation all about us. It just comes naturally. Part of growing up and maturing should train us to think differently about ourselves. But no matter how much you learn and grow, selfishness can be a constant battle.

I remember the counselor, at an appointment months before, saying, "You do realize that this is not your pregnancy, that this is not your life. This is Lindsay's life. You do realize that, right?"

The flash of anger I felt was a strong indication that maybe after all of these years, I had allowed dysfunction to take root, my life to become too intertwined with my daughters' lives. I fired back at the counselor, "It sure feels like my life when I'm the one attending CPO meetings, shopping for maternity clothes, and making sure that prenatal vitamins are being taken!"

I was immediately embarrassed at the bitterness of my tone. She had hit a nerve, a deep nerve. She had hit on a childhood vow that I had made myself years before, a vow that my daughters would come to like me, not just love me. Lives too intertwined? My identity too wrapped up in my mothering? I did my best to answer as the counselor continued to gently ask her probing questions.

A Visit from Brad

Phone calls were made and throughout the next couple of hours those family and friends closest to Lindsay would appear, deposit well wishes, and offer a few last-minute words of encouragement before she gradually went into labor. The nurse came in, took Lindsay's blood pressure, and fussed with the clean white sheets. Meanwhile, Brad arrived in his pressed dress pants and light blue oxford shirt, straight from a long workday.

How many times had I seen this faithful father supporting his girls in the middle of battling the challenges of being the sole financial provider for our family? Time and time again he would leave his office in the middle of the day to insure that his daughters would never have a memory of an empty chair in the audience of their childhood plays. From camping trips to father-daughter banquets, this man was a strong, consistent presence in their lives. But this wasn't a simple dance recital or a free-spirited cheerleading event. This was the biggest event we had ever been through as a family, and once again, he was right on time.

"How you feeling, Linz? You are going to do great. I'm so proud of you," he said as he patted Lindsay's knee with his large fatherly hand. I wanted to jump up from my seat and do my best to interpret what was going on between this father and daughter I loved so much. It was like I knew and could understand both of their languages. I could understand what they meant to say in their hearts that for some reason they had trouble expressing to each other. Over the years, sincere sentiments and messages of love had simply gotten lost in translation between the two.

I was the only one in the world who was aware of all the times that we had laid awake, long after the lights had been turned off, whispering, "You still awake?"

"Yep."

"Can't sleep?"

"Nope."

"Me neither."

On one of those "stare at the ceiling" kind of nights I grabbed his hand tightly and offered the encouragement, "You are a good dad, Brad. Don't you see that she is picking a dad for her little girl who is like her own daddy?" He whispered, "Yeah, I guess so." I continued, "Lindsay told me that when the counselor asked her what kind of childhood she wanted for her baby, she said, 'The same as mine.'"

Lindsay—JOY Comes in the Morning

Kinley Joy was born with a soft cry at 6:49 in the morning after about 15 minutes of hard labor and only four pushes. During delivery my mom was right there next to me holding one of my legs while Bethany held the other. The doctor was so calm; it was almost like she did this for a living! I was so happy! The minute I saw Kinley I was reminded of the verse in the book of Psalms. After all the sorrow and pain that lasted through the night, Kinley JOY came in the morning! (Psalm 30:5). She weighed 7 pounds 6 ounces and was 19¼ inches long. Her APGAR score was 9.9. She was perfect! She was my perfect baby.

They placed her on my chest, and she was the most amazing thing I had ever seen. Of course I couldn't help but cry. I couldn't believe how perfect she was and how much I loved her. There was so much joy, not only in the room around me, but also in my heart. The joy seemed to swallow up any lingering sorrow that there might have been. Now all that mattered was Kinley Joy. She was here and she was perfection.

Several days before we'd made a "birth plan" so we'd all know what was going to happen, who would be in the room, and when they'd be there. In our plan we said that I would hold Kinley first, then Bryan and I would get some time to be in the room alone to talk to the baby and say our good-byes. But as it turned out, we scrapped the plan. There was so much joy and happiness that I didn't need that time alone.

I felt good about our decision to put Kinley up for adoption, and I no longer felt like she was being taken away from me. Bryan held her, and then Bethany, and then the rest of the family who was in the waiting room came in—my dad, Jeff, and Bryan's mom. It was all very exciting. The room was filled with life and joy, tears and laughter, all because a little baby was born that Saturday morning. All the fights, anger, uncertainty, confusion, and pain were gone. We were celebrating new life!

Once they moved me out of delivery and into my own room, I was available to see visitors the rest of the day. That was the best thing about delivery early on a Saturday morning; everyone was off work and able to come by to see Kinley; my friends from high school who were still in town, Jeff and Bethany's friends, my parents' friends, and all my extended family. Each person was thrilled to finally meet her, and I was so proud to show her off. I was also blessed with a little alone time with her during one of the few times when the room emptied out. I loved getting to be with her just holding her close. I could not stop smiling as I stared at her, memorizing every inch of her perfect face. Looking down at Kinley, there was no doubt, this little baby was a miracle straight from God. I was overwhelmed by people's love, time, and gifts.

That night after everyone had left, it was just me and my mom and Kinley in the room. I was in the bed holding Kinley with my mom lying next to me. It was such a sweet time for the three of us to be alone together. Even now, the memory of that moment makes me smile. We had made it. My mom and I had made it through the hardest journey of our lives and now we were able to hold a beautiful baby girl in our arms. We talked about Kinley and about how happy we were. We took lots of pictures of her, analyzing everything about her from her little toes to her perfectly lined lips. It was the best day of my life.

Getting to spend that quiet time with little Kinley Joy was worth every second of the last 40 weeks of pregnancy. Sure, God brought me Joy, but He also brought me a joy I didn't even know was possible. I did it. I was a mother, a very happy and grateful mother, with a precious baby girl.

The next morning I was cleared to check out of the hospital, and Kinley was able to go home with Bethany and Jeff. They would be leaving a little bit earlier because Bryan and I were delayed by all the paperwork we had to fill out.

Before Jeff and Bethany left the hospital, they brought Kinley into my room to say good-bye. Kinley was dressed in a sweet outfit that I had bought for her and she looked beautiful. I held her close and said my good-byes before they put her in the carrier headed to their car.

I will never forget the memory of watching them leave the hospital room with Kinley in the carrier, facing backwards in my direction. I started to cry as they made their way out of my room with their new baby in tow. This was the big event I'd been dreading ever since I made the decision to place my baby up for adoption. I was officially no longer Kinley's mom. Jeff and Bethany had THEIR baby, and now all I was left with was the paperwork declaring that I was the birth mom and Bryan was the birth dad. I felt a sense of emptiness as they walked out the door.

I didn't regret the decision because I knew Kinley was getting the best parents possible, but that didn't mean I wasn't sad. I wanted to be her mom so badly, but I knew this was no time for selfishness; I had to do what was right for my baby. I had learned that being a mom meant having to put my child's needs and well-being above my own.

It took us about an hour, but we finally got the paperwork completed; and it was finally my turn to leave the hospital. My mom wheeled me in a wheelchair to the elevator and down to the car in the parking garage. It was a lonely ride … just the two of us heading home without a baby.

Looking back on that day I can see how God often uses the trials we go through to bring us closer to Him. He doesn't cause the trials; trials are a natural part of living in this world. Jesus told us, "In this world you will have trouble. But take heart! I have overcome the world" (John 16:33).

But God uses those inevitable trials to make us more Christlike and purify our hearts through each and every difficult time we encounter. He's faithful to use those difficult times to our good, even when the trials are caused by our own sin.

I left the hospital that day a different person. Not only was I a mother, I was a much stronger woman, a woman who had just been promoted to the next level of life. No longer was I the immature, arrogant, "I'm in charge of my own life" teenager. I was now a wiser woman whose will was surrendered to God.

If we can grasp this new perspective on our trials, we can walk through them in a more mature, more courageous way, standing taller than we did when we walked into them. In this context, this verse is easier to understand: "Consider it pure joy, my brothers and sisters, whenever you face trials of many kinds, because you know that the testing of your faith produces perseverance" (James 1:2-3).

CHAPTER 27

Lindsay

BACK TO "NORMAL" LIFE

O nce home from the hospital, my mom insisted that I take things slow and just sit on the couch and watch television the whole week until school started. I needed to rest and recover, not only physically, but emotionally as well. I remember that the Summer Olympics was on, so I ended up watching sports that I didn't even know were sports!

But after several days on the couch I was antsy and more than ready for school to start. I showed up to first day of community college with a tight sports bra on to keep my milk from leaking out. I had a full milk supply but no baby to nurse.

It was difficult to get my mind wrapped around how I could show up for school on the first day with no one having a clue that I'd had a baby just the week before. Honestly, that was the weirdest thing. I had just gone through the physical trauma of giving birth and going through the emotional trauma of giving my baby away, and yet no one at school was even the least bit aware. I'd had this major, life-altering event and these people were oblivious.

Strangely enough, it felt exactly like when I first found out I was pregnant. Before I started showing, I could deny the whole situation and pretend to everyone that I was normal, but inside I was dying. Now I was doing my best to attend classes and focus on school, but it felt like my left arm was cut off and no one could see it. It was like the past nine months had never even happened, like I'd been to war and come back and just dropped into society. I had never felt so out of place. I felt like screaming to all the busy people with their backpacks on and their ear buds in and their heads down, rushing back and forth on campus, "DO YOU KNOW WHAT JUST HAPPENED TO ME?" I felt like grabbing them by the shoulders, getting in their face and yelling, "DO YOU KNOW THAT THEY TOOK MY BABY?"

But no, I couldn't yell, I couldn't show my true feelings, I couldn't grab anyone. I had to act normal. I had to push my feelings down and keep them bottled up inside. It always makes me wonder how many other people I pass every single day who are trying to blend in and be normal when in reality their world is crashing in around them.

We see these people every day who are doing a great job of faking it. They look like things are going great and that they haven't got a care in the world. Meanwhile, they might have just lost a loved one, or just found out that their spouse has been cheating on them, or maybe they've just learned that they have cancer. It's a great reminder to all of us to be kind … to everyone we meet. It only takes an ounce of effort to smile at a stranger or offer a simple compliment or word of encouragement that might interrupt their current pain with a ray of light and hope. I would like to think that we can all be a little more like Jesus to everyone we encounter, giving them a glimpse of Him. All it takes is the will to venture out of our personal little bubbles to see people the way Jesus sees them … with eyes of love, acceptance, and grace.

Life Goes On

That's how the next year of my life went. I wasn't just feeling weird and awkward my first week of college. I was trying to figure out how to carry on with my life for a full year after I had Kinley. I had to keep telling myself to be normal, just be normal. I continued to grieve the loss of my baby, constantly crying, missing her so much. Often I would break down sobbing, thinking, *This is relentless. When will the pain stop?* I thought I had experienced deep pain when I was in labor, but this emotional heartache was much deeper than the physical pain I went through. Looking back, I can see that I was struggling with an emotional longing to know my baby.

The pain was ruthless, but I kept walking in confidence that my God had not forsaken me, that He hadn't left my side, that He was still there right next to me every step of the way. I knew that He would follow through on His promise to take care of my baby and me. I knew that while I might be dealing with unbearable pain, I was not alone. He was holding me close, He saw all my tears, and not only did He just see them, He collected them; they were precious to Him (Psalm 56:8). I could sense His comforting voice in my heart telling me that I had made the right decision and that everything would be okay.

I was so blessed that Bethany let me see Kinley whenever my mom babysat Kinley and Reese, which was usually once a week. Seeing Kinley on a regular basis helped numb the pain. She was growing up so quickly, but getting to see her almost every week allowed me to feel like I wasn't missing out on as much.

However, my heart and mind were still filled with all-consuming grief, grief that not only kept me up at night but filled my mind with doubts and confusion during the day. It was in the midst of all this that Bryan and I realized that we didn't have much in common anymore. We finally ended our relationship about a month after Kinley was born.

During my first semester at the community college, I attended a discipleship program led by my mom. It was a very intensive time of renewal and seeking the Lord for me. It was through this group that I rediscovered my identity in Christ and started to experience true healing for all my hurt and pain. I learned that surrender isn't a "once and done" thing. Surrender needs to happen every day, maybe multiple times a day. Our flesh will continue to rise up like a weed growing in an untended garden. We lay down our pain, but then find ourselves picking it up again. I thought I'd surrendered to God, but I surrendered again and gave all I had to the Lord, including my relationship with Bryan.

The Bible says, "Who may stand in his holy place? The one who has clean hands and a pure heart…" (Psalm 24:3-4). When our hands are clean, it means they are open, not clutching and grabbing, holding on tight to things we have no business hanging on to. When we approach God, we need to fully surrender and let go of the things we're holding on to so tightly. Only then will our hearts be pure and we can find peace and healing in Him.

It was in the process of that surrender that I was able to receive healing from all the hurt and all the emotional connections that I'd had with my baby's birth father. Spiritually, I had finally started to get things back on the right track.

Scarlet—Kinley Goes Home with Bethany

It was a week after Kinley had gone home with her new family, and my mind started feeling like when the anesthesia wears off after a dental procedure. The dentist gives you a shot of Novocain in your gums so they're numb to the deep drilling that has to take place. It's painless at the time, but gradually your lip starts to tingle and then the medication wears off and the pain finally sets in, revealing just how deep the extraction has been.

My Novocain injection started as soon as Kinley Joy sucked the air of this world into her lungs. Lindsay had carried precious Kinley for nine months and as she came out into this world, I watched, giggled, and breathed a sigh of relief as she was transferred over to her new mother— the mother who would raise her forever.

Yes, my shot of Novocain was full of painless elation while we were at the hospital, but now that we were home the painful heartache was beginning to make itself known. My soul was grieving. Kinley was no longer ours. Sure, she was safe and sound, and just across town with people we knew and loved, but she was no longer under our roof or in our care.

And I wasn't the only one hurting. In a bedroom upstairs was a heartbroken young mother, a mother who had made a difficult decision, which just happened to be the very best decision for her daughter. But now she was feeling the enormous grief of that difficult choice, weeping off and on, longing to hold her child.

Although her conception surprised us all, I understood spiritually that Kinley's Heavenly Father had her in His plan from the beginning of time. She was not a surprise to Him. Her story would be told, and unborn babies would be rescued as their teen mothers read Kinley's redemptive story. *Would Kinley know the weight of her life? Were we putting too much pressure and expectation on this child? Would other kids tease her because she was adopted?* My thoughts would twirl and swirl. There was no mistaking the fact that God had ordained Kinley's birth. But I was beginning to sense that her birth had an even greater purpose. It was beginning to make sense to me why, early on, God guided us to Habakkuk 2:2 which says, "Then the Lord replied: 'Write down the revelation and make it plain on tablets so that a herald may run with it.'" The Lord led us all throughout the pregnancy to write this story down ... so others could hear it and read it and be encouraged.

One night during this time I had a dream—a dream that had only one scene. I saw Kinley as a 17 year old, sound asleep, lying on her back. She looked like a sleeping princess, like one you might see illustrated in a book of fairy tales. She had long brown hair that had a slight wave to it as it cascaded off her pillow and flowed down the side of her bed.

As she slept I was able to notice that she shared Bethany's beautiful features. I saw that in her right hand she held a massive golden sword with a handle that had been inlaid with large jewels. The weight of the sword caused her right arm to hang down off the edge of the bed. She wore a heavy gown that was made of rich green velvet, like you would see worn by royalty. In the dream I felt myself reach out for her, just wanting to take her up in my arms and hold her closely and show her how much I loved her.

When I woke up I immediately knew the interpretation of the dream as I felt God speak to my heart. He told me to let her sleep. This was not her time, but when the time was right, she would wake up and be a warrior princess for Him. I was reminded that in nature, there's always a period of time between when you plant the seed and when you can expect the harvest. A farmer doesn't go out to plant one day and expect to harvest the very next day. His calendar is in seasons. There are seasons of planting, seasons of waiting, then seasons of harvesting.

The same is true in God's Kingdom. There's often a season of time that takes place between when we pray and when we see the answer to that prayer. Sometimes we don't see the answer of a prayer immediately because it takes time to develop.

In my dream, Kinley was already armed with the sword even though she wasn't ready to use it yet. That would come in another season. The Lord cautioned me against obsessing over Kinley, overthinking, and worrying about her future. He told me that it was time for me to focus on my own race. He said it was time for Lindsay and me to fight our own battles to take the land that He's called us to take.

I knew instinctively that Kinley was being formed and raised under Bethany's godly mothering and that's why, in the dream, she had taken on Bethany's features.

For the weeks that followed, whenever I was tempted to be fearful about Kinley's future I would remind myself that it wasn't her time yet, it was her season to sleep. I had the confidence that she was being nurtured and loved and was thriving right where she was. I had to jolt myself time and time again to not miss this season of my own life. I couldn't afford to allow myself to be constantly distracted by the sleeping warrior princess. Like Esther, I needed to focus on doing what God had called me to do "for such a time as this" (Esther 4:14).

Rock-a-Bye Kinley

My nose was filled with the sweet scent of baby shampoo as I rocked my six-month-old granddaughter. We rocked rhythmically to the swish-swish of her sound machine that kept her from waking her big sister. Reese was sleeping peacefully in her own crib just on the other side of the wall from where we rocked in the wee hours of the morning. Jeff and Bethany were away for the weekend, and I had the privilege of babysitting. As I gave Kinley her first bottle of the day, my heart was overflowing with thankfulness. I was thankful that God had placed this precious little girl in this safe, loving home and thankful that I was allowed to be part of her life.

When Lindsay first told us that she was pregnant on that unforgettable Saturday morning, I could have never imagined how this story would have unfolded. Now here I sat, looking into Kinley's dark brown eyes, hearing her suck her bottle and holding her tiny body in my arms. *God is faithful, God is faithful, God is faithful,* my heart declared in harmony with the rhythmic tempo of the chair rocking back and forth.

As I looked down at my sweet, precious granddaughter, it occurred to me that this story wasn't ending, it was just beginning! As each day unfolded in Kinley's life, we were reminded of how much bigger God's plans are for our lives than we could imagine. I bet Moses never imagined that he would one day lead the Hebrews out of Egypt. I'm sure that before God told him, Abraham couldn't have imagined that he would be the father of many nations. Or Esther, do you think she imagined that she would be responsible for saving the entire Hebrew nation from execution? What about the disciples? Peter, John, Matthew, James, and the others, did they know what they were getting into when they responded to Christ's call on their lives? Could Paul have dreamed while sitting in a jail cell scratching out letters of instruction and encouragement to the churches he'd planted, that we'd be reading his words over 2,000 years later? The fact is, God grabbed all these people out of relative obscurity and gave them a much larger mission, a cause that was much greater than anything they could imagine.

Kinley had already brought immense joy to so many people, so much more than we could have ever imagined … and she was just getting started. I was confident then, and still am today, that God will love and shape Kinley into the young woman He intends her to be, specifically designed to fulfill her calling in this world. And you're the same way. You might not think so, but God has a plan for you too. And it's a plan that's way bigger than you might think. It's so big that you won't even be able to accomplish it without His help and guidance. Like Kinley, God has created you for great things!

Lindsay

I continued to attend counseling after Kinley was born. It was through counseling that I was able to talk things out and have someone help me process all that was going on in my life. Through medication, help from the Lord, and getting mentored from many women, including my Aunt Jana, I was almost back to normal. I was starting to hear from the Lord again and things were becoming much more clear.

That next January I started school at Oral Roberts University in Tulsa. I tried my best to enjoy living in the dorms but found that it was extremely hard to fit in. I felt like the girls on my floor were so immature and I couldn't help but think, *If you only knew the adult choices I've had to make … if you only knew the depth of the pain I have felt.* It was hard for me to connect with the other students, but I knew I had to just keep seeking Christ. I had to keep walking in obedience, doing what He asked me to do. I had to trust Him.

It was during this time that I was set up on a date with an older guy who was a friend of my cousin. I had no intention of dating anyone. In fact, I'd already made the decision that if I ever let another guy get close enough to be my boyfriend that I would marry him. After everything I had dealt with in the last year, I didn't feel like having a fling with some immature college boy.

The guy I was set up with was named Malachi. I had known who he was but had never met him or even really talked to him. He was good-looking and about five years older than me. After my cousin set things up, Malachi texted me to make the final arrangements … I'll admit I was nervous.

At the appointed time, Malachi picked me up; and I ended up going on the best first date of my life. We went to dinner downtown and then ice-skating. The date was perfect. We had so many things in common so we had a lot to talk about. I remember laughing more than I had in months.

From that first date, I could tell he was sweeping me off my feet. I couldn't believe things were going so well. On our second date I gathered up my courage and told him all about Kinley. I wanted him to know my full story at the beginning before emotions got involved. It turned out that he already knew about the baby because of my cousin, but I could tell it was still a difficult story for him to listen to ... and to process. Malachi had always wanted to have a healthy marriage so he had been faithful to save himself for his future wife. He truly loved the Lord and wanted to live a life that was pleasing to Him.

We continued to date and work through the issues that emerged as our relationship progressed. Although Malachi and I had a lot to work through, the process made us stronger. But it wasn't all hard work and pain; we had plenty of times filled with joy and laughter.

In a very real way, building a relationship with Malachi was good therapy for me. He started becoming an integral part of my healing process. His unconditional love and acceptance flooded my broken heart like healing oil. He was a constant presence, always there to hold me as I cried; accompanying me through the difficult healing process. He demonstrated what true love really is, the unconditional love of Christ. Malachi loved me regardless of what I had done. In the Bible, the name Malachi means "my messenger" or "my angel," and Malachi was my angel with God's message of love for me.

I felt like God told me, "Malachi is the reward for your obedience concerning Kinley." God was right and I was so blessed to marry that man just nine short months after our first date and only one month after Kinley's first birthday.

Through my experiences, I've learned that my past mistakes do not define my future. The enemy's strategy was to hold me down, mired in my past, feeling like a dirty high schooler for the rest of my life. But I learned that I am who He says I am, not who the devil says I am. He calls me "fallen" and "sinner," "dirty" and "ashamed." But God calls me His child (Galatians 4:7), and His new creation (2 Corinthians 5:17). I am God's masterpiece, His workmanship created to do good things (Ephesians 2:10 NLT).

But this knowledge did not come easily. I had walked through fire and learned how to fight to keep the devil from gaining a foothold in my life. I found victory by learning to accept God's truth instead of the devil's lies. I accepted the fact that Christ had already won the battle when He died on the cross and rose again.

I've learned that your sin, no matter how terrible, isn't strong enough to erase what Christ accomplished on the cross. I want to encourage you to walk in the freedom of all God has for you. You are all that God says you are!

In my case, even though I had sinned and fallen short, He forgave me and presented me with the gift of an amazing daughter and a loving, healthy home for her to be raised in. The icing on the cake was that God also gave me a husband who loves God with all his heart. Don't let the enemy steal your God-given blessings by miring you in your past.

CHAPTER 28

Scarlet

A FINAL WORD

often think back to the church service where God asked me to give Lindsay up to Him … completely. It was a year before her pregnancy so I had no idea why He was asking me to release her to Him. I felt like I was laying her on the altar and every maternal instinct I had fought to hold on to her. It really was a messy, emotional process to give her up. But in that service as I struggled, God gave me a vision. I could see myself wrapping a package that I knew represented Lindsay. Together, God and I folded and taped brown paper around the package, getting it ready to be sent off and mailed. We covered the brown paper in little pink heart stickers.

At the time I had no idea what this meant, but now I see that Lindsay is a prepared package sent out to the world, a package that proclaims the Pro-Life message, bringing joy and hope to the pregnant teenager. She is a package that blesses adopted children and explains to them what a birth mother's sacrificial heart feels for her child, a feeling that never goes away. And on a larger scale, Lindsay is a package of hope for all of us.

Yes, Lindsay has been launched into changing so many lives. And remember those little pink heart stickers on the package? I could've never imagined what they meant until five years later when I found myself in Kinley's pre-K classroom surrounded by her four-year-old classmates. It was Valentine's Day and by this time in the school year her teacher was used to the full entourage of Kinley's fan club being around. We had been there for every event that the school allowed us to attend. All of us together, Bryan's mom, Jeff and Bethany, Brad and me, Bethany's parents, and Brad's parents gathered with all our love and support focused on precious Kinley Joy.

Our presence painted a beautiful picture of open adoption. By now we were used to answering questions from other parents about how we were all related to Kinley. This party didn't seem any different than the others except for the moment when I told Kinley good-bye. She unexpectedly shoved a little pink sticker onto my white blouse right at her height where my belly was and proclaimed, "I love you, Mimi!" How could I have ever known the absolute joy that this little girl, my little pink heart girl, would bring to my life? God sure has a way of showing off.

A Final Word from Lindsay

By this time, you're probably thinking, *What happened next? How did all the uncertainties work out?* Well, first of all, I no longer live in a state of uncertainty. I live in a state of Faith. I may not be certain about all things in my life, but I have faith that God is looking out for me and will take care of me no matter what.

The grief started to get better soon after Kinley made it to her first birthday. The old saying, "Time heals all wounds" really was true in my case. The more time that passed, the better I felt. But not a day goes by that her precious face doesn't float up in my mind causing a smile to cross my face.

A common question I'm asked is how often I get to see her and the truth is ... not nearly enough; I could see that little girl every single day! For the first four years of her life, I was able to see her almost every week.

Seeing her is like getting a shot of caffeine directly to my brain. She fills my heart with so much joy, and I know that I know that I know that I made the right decision and picked the right parents for Kinley. Jeff and Bethany have been amazing parents and have always been open to letting me see her. I know she has the perfect family now.

Little Kinley is now the middle child of three girls (just like me!) and is full of laughter. She never wants for anything, and it blesses me to know that she is right where she needs to be. Just the little things like seeing her play with her sisters show me that she already has a better life than the one I could have provided for her.

This little girl is smart and creative. She is always asking questions and coming up with her own ideas and plans. She is already showing the early qualities of a leader. Her middle name, Joy, could not fit her better. She lives life to the fullest and is continually filled with excitement and wonder. Kinley has a way of giving me a look that just melts my heart, and I can easily see Christ's faithfulness in her eyes. I know that we have a special bond when I hear her joyfully yell my name whenever I knock on the door to her home. She calls me "Lala," and she runs to give me a giant hug and tells me that she missed me.

Bethany has been wonderful to allow Kinley to know her story before she could even talk. Kinley has never been lied to and knows her story is different than her two sisters. I got an amazing and surreal surprise when Kinley was two years old and Bethany asked her, "Who's belly did you come out of?" With a giant grin on her tiny little face, she lifted her finger and pointed at me and screamed "Lala's"! Then she went back to playing again, just as simple as that. Kinley knows her story. No lies, just love.

Don't get me wrong, there are still days, even five years later that are hard. I still feel an empty spot in my heart, but I know that God has a plan and a purpose for Kinley's life. God has allowed me to use my experience and brokenness to connect with others, and I know He will use Kinley to do the same. The Bible assures us that we overcome by the blood of the Lamb and by the word of [our] testimony (Revelation 12:11).

That's how powerful our testimony, our story, is. It has the power to defeat the devil and all his lies. When we are vulnerable enough to share our story with others, it disarms the enemy and renders his lies powerless. People can argue doctrine and they can argue theology, but no one can argue with your story … it's YOUR STORY! And that's what makes it such a powerful weapon in your hand.

I'm committed to share my story to bring freedom to those still held captive by the same sin and shame that held me. I know that my story of redemption can bring freedom to others.

As Kinley continues to grow and move on with her life, so do I. I graduated college in three years with the highest honor, thanks to my 3.8 GPA. I didn't let my situation define my outcome. I've decided that staying in depression would delete all of the sacrifices that I have made so I continue to challenge myself to make the most of what I've been through.

I'm so blessed that God called me out of the darkness. I am a strong woman in Christ, and I know that if I had the strength to give up my baby, I have the strength to do anything God calls on me to do. I am a warrior!

I have a full-time sales job that I love. In 2016 God called Malachi and me to move away from Tulsa. Moving away from Kinley was very hard for me, but I knew that I had to live my life … and she had to live hers. I couldn't pass up this opportunity by choosing to stay stuck in the past. Moving away was my way of moving on. But make no mistake, I continue to FaceTime her and come to Tulsa for a visit every chance I get.

Being married has been one of the most fulfilling journeys of my life. I have a true life partner in Malachi. He's been someone who has never stopped loving me and has always taken good care of me. We laugh often, have a true friendship, and we celebrate Kinley's life just like we do almost everything else … together! By obeying God and placing Kinley up for adoption, it has allowed both her and me to live the lives that God has called us to live.

Was a teen pregnancy an easy journey? No. Do I recommend premarital sex, along with all its heartaches, whether there's a baby or not? Definitely not. But I wouldn't change my story for anything in the world. I love that baby more than anyone could ever imagine. I'm continually praying for her.

If you ever find yourself, or someone you love in my shoes, please know that there is hope. No matter what your battle is, sex, drugs, addiction, disease, unforgiveness, hate, or loss, God has a purpose and a plan for your life. And His purpose and plan stay true whether you caused your current negative circumstances or not.

You are not too far gone to be redeemed! I want to say that again to make sure you got it. You are not too far gone to be redeemed by God. No matter what you've done, you have not gone beyond His reach to pull you back. He loves you and is pursuing you to bring you back to life.

Jesus Himself gives us this encouragement, "What do you think? If a man owns a hundred sheep, and one of them wanders away, will he not leave the ninety-nine on the hills and go to look for the one that wandered off? And if he finds it, truly I tell you, he is happier about that one sheep than about the ninety-nine that did not wander off" (Matthew 18:12-13).

No matter what the enemy might be telling your heart, you cannot sin too much or fall so far that you'll lose God's love. You cannot mess up so much that there is no way to get your life back on track. There is freedom in Christ Jesus! All He wants is your heart. You can trust Him. He never disappoints and never leaves your side. The Apostle Paul wrote it down like this, "For I am convinced that neither death nor life, neither angels nor demons, neither the present nor the future, nor any powers, neither height nor depth, nor anything else in all creation, will be able to separate us from the love of God that is in Christ Jesus our Lord" (Romans 8:38-39).

I know I can trust that the Lord will take care of Kinley just like He took care of Moses, Samuel, Esther, and His own Son, Jesus. There are some amazing adoption stories in the Bible demonstrating that God takes special care of those who have been adopted. Remember, our sin may have separated us from God, but our Heavenly Father has adopted us all. God also takes care of the mother's heart because He had to give up His own baby too.

Probably one of the most well-known verses in the Bible says, "For God so loved the world that he gave his one and only Son, that whoever believes in him shall not perish but have eternal life" (John 3:16).

I'm sure we've all read that verse and heard it thousands of times; you've probably even memorized it. Whenever I used to read that verse I would focus on the second phrase, "that he gave his one and only Son...." That's such a statement of sacrifice, and it should set the example for all of us.

But I've learned that perhaps the most important part of that verse is the very first phrase. It's the most important part because it's the WHY of John 3:16. Why did God sacrifice His Son? Why did God choose to reconcile humanity with Himself? Why did God forgive your sins and redeem your soul? The answer is found in the first few words of the verse: "For God so loved the world...." His love covers us, redeems us, heals us, and delivers us.

We've all heard the story Jesus told of the prodigal son (Luke 15:11-32). It's the story of a man who had two sons. One of them wanted his share of his inheritance early, so his father gave it to him; and the son took his money, packed up, and left home. Over time, the son squandered all the money on loose living. A drought came on the land, and the son became desperate. He decided to go back home and beg his father to have him back, not as a son, but as a servant. He began his journey back, dreading the confrontation, humiliation, and embarrassment that would happen when he finally saw his father.

But the story turns in verse 20 where it says, "But while he was still a long way off, his father saw him and was filled with compassion *for him; he* ran to his son, threw his arms around him and kissed him." The father, who was watching daily for his son to return, ran to meet him and welcomed him with open arms, back as a precious son and not as a servant.

Like the father in the story, our God is a good Father who loves us and redeems us and brings us into His family no matter what we've done or how far we've fallen. I hope you'll never forget His promise in Psalm 30:5 NKJV: "Weeping may endure for a night..." but Joy *will* come!

CHAPTER 29

Bethany's Story
THE DREAM

closed my eyes and there she was again. This little girl had filled my dreams and prayers from the time I was a child. She sat alone in the church on the second pew, staring intently at me. Her dark complexion complimented the brown hair that fell in soft curls over her shoulders. She wore a sweet dress and donned a big bow in her beautiful hair; she was no more than three or four years old. I was standing on the stage looking at her. I couldn't take my eyes off this tiny doll sitting alone on the second row. Neither of us ever said a word, but I knew in my heart I would help her someday.

I mentioned this little girl in the first entry of my very first journal. It was May of 1999. I was only 13 years old, and while it might have been my first written memory of her, I had been seeing her in my dreams for years.

A Bolt of Lightning

Early one Saturday morning many years later, I woke up around 6:00 a.m. to the sounds of my little girl crying. This was my signal. Reese was hungry again. So I stumbled out of bed and across the hall to her nursery. The sunlight was beginning to creep through the shades of her window, and it seemed as though it was going to be a day like any other—a day filled with feedings and diaper changes, giggles and tummy time, but then Jeff walked through the nursery door. Sleepy-eyed, he lay down on the floor next to me. I knew something was wrong. I could see it in his eyes; they were sad.

"Lindsay is pregnant."

The news hit me like a bolt of lightning. I can still hear the words echoing inside my head. *Lindsay? Our niece? The one in high school? No, it couldn't be. I must have heard that wrong.* I sat motionless in shock. There were so many things flashing through my mind, but the only things I could manage to say were, "How far along is she?" and "What's going to happen to the baby?" Jeff let me know she was already six months along, and they were putting this little girl up for adoption ... *this little girl.*

Maybe it was because I was holding our precious baby girl in my arms, but the moment he said those words it struck a chord. I'm sure he told me more, but I couldn't process it. The thoughts in my head were spinning, but none of them would come out.

Being a part of such a large family, I assumed someone had already offered to adopt the baby. Then I found out that not only had no one offered, no one but her immediate family even knew she was pregnant until the night before. It was like something inside clicked, a light bulb came on, and in that instant, I knew this was *our* baby.

Jeff and I spent the next hour discussing what adopting this little girl might look like and how it could affect our family. Would they even want someone in the family to adopt this child? I couldn't imagine how I would feel if I were in that situation. For the rest of my life, I would have to see someone else raising my child. No, if moving on was what Lindsay needed, it would be much easier for her to choose someone outside of family to adopt her child. Every ounce of logic I possessed said, "This is crazy! You already have a baby!" but my heart kept telling me to fight.

We waited a day or two before letting Brad and Scarlet know about our willingness to adopt. We wanted to see if anything changed in our spirit, but instead of hesitation I just felt a greater sense of urgency. We knew there was a timetable in place and felt that they needed to know what options were available to them. I just wanted to make sure we were on their list.

Knowing you have absolutely no control can be completely unnerving and totally peaceful at the same time. I like to be able to easily manage my life, but in this situation I HAD to step back and say, "God, if this is Your will, YOU will have to do it all. I cannot control the outcome." I knew at that point I had to trust God, step back, and rest in Him.

When we felt like the time was right, Jeff called his brother Brad (Lindsay's dad) to let him know what was on our heart. Our offer seemed to take everyone by surprise. It was no secret that our transition into parenthood had not been an easy one. Reese had only just recently begun sleeping for any significant amount of time, and now we were offering to start this whole process over again with zero respite. Jeff and Brad set a date for the four of us to meet and discuss the possibility in more detail.

Next Steps

A week later we sat down with Brad and Scarlet to pretend that any of us had an idea what we were getting ourselves into. Understandably, they wanted to make sure we were serious about our offer before having us meet with Lindsay. We had nothing concrete to offer anyone except the knowledge that God told us to do this. But God made it incredibly clear to our hearts from the beginning that our act of obedience was NOT in adopting this child, because that was not something we could control.

Our single act of obedience was in *offering* to adopt this precious baby. We assured them that we were 100 percent serious with zero chance of changing our minds.

Now that our offer was out there, all that was left for Jeff and me was to sit back and wait to hear what was going to happen next. We were keenly aware that at any point they could say no, but we also knew that at any point they could say yes. The clock was ticking until this precious baby would be here, and I had no idea what I needed to do, so we just continued to wait.

While we waited, we continued to pray. We wanted to make sure every step we took was in line with God's will. We wanted to cement this decision in our hearts so that when people questioned it, we could say with complete certainty that this is what God called us to do. For once in my life, I knew I had acted in instant obedience, and that for the rest of her life, we could tell our little girl that we wanted her from the moment we found out she existed. We knew God made her just for us, and even though her entrance into this world might not have been planned by her birth parents, God has His own plan. He made her for us and her story will save the lives of many others. She was going to live so that others may live.

Time to Tell My Family

Jeff's family now all knew about this upcoming bundle of joy and had heard of our offer to adopt this baby girl, but my family was still in the dark. My parents were coming to town only a week later, and I planned on telling them in person. But the more I thought about it, the more I realized I might need to give them some time to process rather than blindsiding them and expecting them to be excited.

So one afternoon, I put Reese down for a nap, plopped myself in a chair on the front porch, and called them. When I asked them to put me on speaker, I knew their growing suspicion would be that we were expecting again and in a sense, I guess we were. I broke the news and we spent the next hour discussing what this possibility could mean for us.

Of course, they had lots of questions, most of which I couldn't answer. The phrase I said most during that two-to-three month period was, "I don't know." I did my best to explain to them what I could. I assured them that we weren't going into this blindly; we understood that at any point the rug could be pulled out from under us and we could end up with no baby at all. But this was something that was not optional for us; this was something we felt we *had* to do. We had to be obedient.

It's a Girl!

It had been about a month since we made our offer to adopt this precious baby. We took the time to meet with both her birth parents and her grandparents and took a careful look into the legal steps required for her adoption. We began to sell off furniture for what would be her nursery. We even inquired about buying a new car to better fit all four of us, and then we waited.

Then one day Lindsay called and asked if she and the birth father could come and see us that evening. I didn't know what to expect, but I knew this was it. One way or another, we were going to get an answer that evening. This little girl was only two months away from being here and the clock was ticking.

I was excited, anxious, and a little overwhelmed. The minutes felt like hours and that entire day dragged on and on. Finally, the time had come, and I was pacing by the front door anxious for them to arrive. Occasionally I would peek through the blinds to see if their car was in sight. Jeff and I waited and waited … and waited.

The doorbell finally rang and my heart skipped a beat. I took one look at Jeff, inhaled deeply, and opened the door. We were met with two smiling faces on the other side of the door, smiling with their mouths, but grieving in their hearts. It still amazes me how God can turn one person's mess into someone else's miracle. But the two stepped into our home carrying a cake box, and we were met with a joyful yet somber greeting. We made our way upstairs, sat down, and after a few moments of silence, we knew what was coming. Tears began to run down Lindsay's face. She held the cake box on her lap, and as she opened the box we could see that inside was a delicate pink and white cake with tiny pink booties on it. The cake read, *"It's a Girl!"*

Lindsay paused, halfheartedly smiled, and with the tears still coming asked us if we would be mommy and daddy to their precious baby girl. My emotional walls were broken in that moment. My normally pleasant but reserved nature disappeared as the tears began to fall and all four of us cried together. No words can do justice to this experience. No amount of gratitude or humility would ever suffice when expressing your appreciation in this set of circumstances. Only tears would do. And on this rare occasion, I had plenty of tears to give.

God had settled in my heart as a child that I would adopt. He gave me dreams and visions, and planned every intricate moment of my life so I could be in this room on this night accepting the wonderfully precious life He created. It was an "Ah ha!" moment for me. I was destined to be right here right now. I was created for this moment, "for such a time as this." I was always meant to be this baby's momma. Now it was official. We were going to be a family of four. In only a few short weeks, OUR baby would arrive.

I wanted to shout it from the rooftops and scream it for the world to hear. But I also wanted to protect Lindsay, and if I'm being honest, I wanted to protect myself. As I prayed and waited through the next couple months, God often reminded me of Mary's response to the awe surrounding the birth of Jesus, "But Mary treasured up all these things and pondered them in her heart" (Luke 2:19).

The verse says she *pondered* them in her heart. She didn't make a spectacle or announce it as they rode through the city streets. Mary carried the Son of God in her womb. She had every reason to tell the world, but she didn't. She kept these special secrets close to her heart. She pondered them. She stood in awe of what God had done, what God had chosen for her to be a part of, and waited for His story to reveal itself.

CHAPTER 30

Bethany

REMEMBERING THE DREAM

don't remember the exact moment it hit me, but I remember one day as I was praying, I flashed back to the little girl from my dream so many years before, sitting in the second pew with the bow in her hair. I hadn't thought of her in years. My only recent recollections had come when I found mentions of her in my old journals.

Immediately I scrambled to find that journal, the first one I had ever written. I have twenty some-odd journals filled with dreams, prayers, sermon notes, and the silly scribbles of an adolescent youth. But this journal was special. It was my very first one. I had a feeling that the words of an innocent thirteen-year-old girl might still speak straight to the heart of this grown woman and remind her that God uses those who open their hearts to Him regardless of their age or experience.

I found this special book on a shelf in my closet and flipped it open to the first entry. I wanted to know exactly what I'd said about this little girl. The words were written in my middle-school, oversized, messy handwriting riddled with spelling errors and grammatical mistakes. But there she was in black and white, the little girl with the dark eyes that I'd dreamed of all those years ago.

The entry detailed the recurring dream I'd had of this little girl sitting on the second pew, her soft, wavy brown hair and big bow. I noted how sweet and innocent she looked sitting there all alone. I ended the entry by saying, "But I know I will be able to help her someday." That day had finally come. I sat on the floor of my closet and wept. It seems only fitting that would be the place where God reminded me of those words, because as a youth I spent much of my time on the floor of my closet locked away, spending time with Him. In fact, I was most certainly sitting on the floor of my closet on the day I wrote those very words in my journal.

I'd found her. This little girl was no longer a dream. She was going to be mine. A promise over thirteen years in the making was coming true. God's voice whispered in my ear, "I always keep My promises."

Challenging Days

We didn't walk into this new season of our life with rose-colored glasses. We knew there would be hospital bills, diapers, and baby food. It was understood that we would be walking right back into sleepless nights, mental and emotional exhaustion, and double the work. We knew there could be hurt and pain involving those we loved, and we had no idea how long it may take for those wounds to heal, or if they ever would. We knew we wanted this adoption to be open to *both* sides of this little girl's biological parents. That, in my mind, was the biggest question mark. I couldn't wrap my head around what this might look like or how we could make it work.

As the weeks passed and more people found out our surprising news, I received the same cautious reminder over and over again, "Are you sure you want to do this? You know this won't be easy."

For years, I have struggled with the side of Christianity that tells us life should be easy, that somehow if we are walking in God's will He won't ask us to leap out of our well intentioned, comfortable bubbles to do His work. Yet the reality is, more often than not, this is exactly what God asks us to do. He asks us to follow His lead and go bravely against the grain. He requires us to set aside convenience and comfort and strive for obedience and impact. Jeff and I both knew it wasn't going to be easy, but we also knew that nothing worth having is easy.

Finding Her Name

Putting doubt and any second thoughts behind me, my mind moved ahead to one of the most important things—finding a name for this precious baby. Yes, that's exactly how I meant to say it, *finding* her name. I knew God had already picked her name, and now it was up to Jeff and me to search it out. When we started the adoption process, Lindsay made sure we knew this decision was up to us, and we took it incredibly seriously.

I couldn't control much of what was happening around me at this time, but this was something I could control. I could help provide this baby girl with a name. I found every list of girl names imaginable, and I searched each one of them intently. I made lists of my favorites, crossed some out and added them back on, but nothing felt right. Then one day I saw it, *Kinley.* It was perfect. It was her name. Now I just had to convince everyone else involved and that started with Jeff.

I shared my idea for the name with Jeff and he readily agreed. Kinley was just the right name. Shortly after Jeff and I talked, Lindsay and I were strolling through the baby store, registering for a few things for the upcoming baby shower. I kept trying to bring up the topic but wasn't sure how. I knew this was something she would want to know, but what if she didn't agree? I eventually mustered up the courage to mention that we had come up with a name. She looked at me eagerly. I took a deep breath and said it. "Kinley."

Lindsay began to smile. Maybe it was my imagination, but I felt like we had a moment right there in the middle of the store, and I felt a weight lift off of my back. I could see in her eyes that she too had a weight lift off of her. She had entrusted us with the honor and privilege of naming this little girl, and God put us all on the same page. "Kinley" means "fair hero, fair warrior, the king's meadow." The name said it all; this was her calling: to fight.

On the day God gave us her name, He also showed me a scripture fitting the name of this warrior baby: "Defend the weak and the fatherless; uphold the cause of the poor and the oppressed. Rescue the weak and the needy; deliver them from the hand of the wicked" (Psalm 82:3-4).

This was not a scripture to define her story. It was a scripture to define her *calling*. It was obvious to me, even before she was born, that her life and her story would be to rescue others.

Finding Her Middle Name

While her first name came relatively easily, we struggled with her middle name. I went back and forth through my original lists. Eventually I settled on the name "May," my middle name. Jeff suggested we use Lindsay's middle name, "Joy," but I wasn't sure how I felt about that idea.

So I enlisted the advice of a few people close to me, people I trusted. All the advice I was given said that giving her Lindsay's middle name was a very kind gesture, but not a good idea. They suggested we would be somehow binding the two of them together unnecessarily instead of allowing this baby to be intertwined with our own family heritage.

In my head that made sense, but in my heart I knew God was asking me for yet another step of obedience. So while it is always wise to listen to sound counsel, in the end you have to trust what God speaks to your own heart. We had made our decision and surprisingly Jeff and I were on the same page.

I called Lindsay with the news, leaving her a quick message to call me back. She returned my call late that night assuming something was wrong. In fact, it was just the opposite. I knew the information could wait but I also knew she would want to know this news as soon as possible. I told her we had decided on Kinley's middle name … "Joy," Lindsay's middle name.

There was silence on the other end of the line, and then I heard her begin to softly cry. All I remember her saying is, "Thank you so much. You have no idea what this means to me."

She was right. I really never could know. I had battled on the inside weighing the opinions of people I respected with what I knew God was asking us to do and decided that obedience is a personal thing. But honestly, in the end, I could not think of someone else I would rather name her after. Lindsay is strong, kind, and compassionate, a woman who puts her trust in God even when it doesn't make sense to her. She chose to give this baby life when it would have been easier and more convenient for her to end Kinley's life and move on. She spent nine long months on her knees believing God would provide a home for this child and a life that she would still get to be involved in. She made the difficult choice to stay in Kinley's life, even though that meant there would be a constant reminder of a relationship she would rather forget and a baby she never wanted to give away. She made choices that perhaps she's not proud of, but she chose to tell her story in the hopes that it would save and encourage the lives of others.

Yes, if my baby girl turns out to be like her, I will be more than proud. In our minds, a middle name seemed like such a small tribute to the woman who chose to give life to this little girl, *our* little girl, and it more than suits her joyful and exuberant personality.

CHAPTER 31

Bethany

A CHANGE OF PLANS

Reese's first birthday had been all planned out. I decided on the theme, *Where the Wild Things Are*. Not only was that her favorite book, but it fit her personality perfectly.

I was grateful for my mom who took the idea and ran with it so I didn't have to worry about a thing. We thought we had everything planned out perfectly. Lindsay wasn't scheduled to be induced until Monday morning. It was a Friday and my parents were on their way to Tulsa from Louisiana. The party would be on Saturday, and then we'd have Sunday to recover. My parents would stay a little longer than their normal weekend visits to meet Kinley and help with Reese. Everything was in order, just the way I like it … until it wasn't anymore.

Lindsay called me Friday afternoon with urgent news. I'm not sure exactly what happened but her induction had been rescheduled. It was no longer on Monday as we had anticipated; it was going to happen *that night!* All I can remember saying in response was, "Okay. Sounds good."

I have no idea what happened in the minutes that followed. I know I called Jeff and my parents. We made the obvious decision to postpone Reese's party because while we believed she wouldn't give birth until Saturday late afternoon or night, we didn't want to risk it or be rushed. At some point, Reese and I made a quick run to Target to get goodies and make a little snack basket for Lindsay. Then before I knew it we were visiting Lindsay in the hospital that night.

The whole process was surreal and much of it truly passed in a blur.

We went home that evening after visiting Lindsay. I got started packing some of what I would need for the hospital, assuming I would have plenty of time in the morning to finish up. I tried to sleep, but there were so many things going through my mind I couldn't. I kept checking my phone, making sure I didn't miss any calls. I hadn't. I finally nodded off sometime around 4:00 a.m., and then, a little after 5:00, my phone rang.

The Call

I awoke to *the Call*. I knew exactly what was happening, Kinley Joy was on her way. The drive to the hospital was a haze. Jeff stayed home with Reese until my parents could arrive, but he wasn't going to be in the delivery room so the urgency wasn't quite the same for him. The only thing I can remember from that drive was the dim sunlight that began to appear on the horizon and the rows of arching metal streetlights hanging over the edge of the interstate. I just kept thinking, *I'm going to get my baby girl today. Is this possible? Is this real?*

I got to the hospital, still in a daze. I parked the car and ran inside as fast as I could. I made it there only minutes before the doctor arrived and less than 20 minutes before our Kinley Joy made her appearance in this world. I'm so thankful I got to be a part of it all. I might not have birthed her myself, but this little miracle was now a part of my family and I was able to witness it. We did nothing to deserve this gift, but God gave her to us anyway. I stood back and marveled at the miracle I'd just been a part of, a mother and father giving up their child as an act of obedience and surrendering to the will of God, for the best interests of this baby girl. The fact that I somehow stood to gain was overwhelming. It made no earthly sense to me, but as I held her for the first time, my tears began to flow.

Within a few minutes after her birth, the crowd in the delivery room grew exponentially as more family arrived to join in the celebration. It was then that Jeff got to hold our new daughter, and it was love at first sight. Kinley Joy was here! She was perfect, and that was all that mattered.

A Surprise Blessing

One of the biggest blessings from God during this transition from a family of three to a family of four was when He allowed me to nurse Kinley. He really outdid Himself! I was just about to begin weaning Reese, when we first considered adopting Kinley. It hit me one day, this could work, and I could actually nurse Kinley! So I continued to nurse Reese until Kinley was born and, without any issues at all, I was able to nurse Kinley for just over a year. It may have seemed like a small thing to anyone else, but to me it was an immeasurable blessing. I didn't have nine months to bond with this baby. I didn't have nine months to even bond with the *idea* of this baby. But God allowed me this special time with her every day, and it was completely seamless.

Less than an hour after our Kinley Joy was born, I got to spend a few minutes with her, just the two of us, as I nursed her for the first time. I gazed into her beautiful brown eyes and examined every tiny finger and toe. She was completely perfect. I stood in awe of the fact that although I did not give her life, I could provide it for her from my own body.

I spent the next 24 hours in the hospital constantly being asked one question, "Are *you* the aunt?" I'm not sure exactly what gave it away; perhaps it was the fact I had obviously not just given birth but I was wearing the "all-access" bracelet, or maybe it was because I wandered the floor at night, able to walk on my own and not wearing a hospital gown.

Regardless of how people knew who I was, our story had preceded us. Jeff and I were able to tell the story over and over again. We were able to share the love of Jesus with hospital staff, nurses, doctors, and even other patients and somehow they acted like we were the heroes. The heroes were actually the two teenagers in the next room facing what was likely the hardest decision they would ever have to face. For us, adopting her was never some sort of sacrificial offering. We never once felt like we were doing anyone a favor. She was our child. She was our gift.

Time to Go Home

When the sun finally rose, we had no desire to stay in the hospital any longer than necessary. The pediatrician gave us the all clear. Our little girl was perfect. The temporary guardianship papers had been signed, and Reese was having a birthday party in just a couple of hours. It was time to go home. It was time to take our baby girl home.

She was ready to face the world. She had been covered in more prayers before her life began than most people would know throughout an entire lifetime. She was saying good-bye to her biological mom and dad and was entering into a life where Jeff and I would be the ones responsible for her little soul. As we picked up her car seat and turned to head for the hospital room door, I felt a joy, a peace, and a love like I'd never known before. But in that exact same moment, I was overwhelmed with a heaviness and a broken heart because I realized that I was walking away with someone else's child. Lindsay chose to give us this baby, but that doesn't mean it was an easy choice. I didn't understand until that moment that it was possible for your heart to be broken and yet so full at the same time.

We headed home to start our new life together and to get ready for a house full of guests. Kinley was born early on a Saturday morning, the exact morning we had scheduled Reese's first birthday party. Needless to say, we changed plans quickly and all of our family and friends understood. But the cake had already been bought and we had family in from out of town to attend. So we decided that the most logical thing to do was to bring our one-day-old daughter home from the hospital, and then host a birthday party for our one-year-old daughter just an hour later. Oh, the things we do when life throws us a curve ball!

As much as I wanted to be the mom who sheltered her baby from every possible thing, this was ultimately a picture of our future that God was giving me. He never intended for us to do any of this alone, and by bringing Kinley into our home, we were not just growing our family by one; we were growing our family exponentially. So we didn't simply bring our baby home, we carried her into a party that hasn't stopped.

CHAPTER 32

Bethany

SHE'S NOT A BABY ANYMORE

At around 18 months, Kinley was finally toddling around. She would make it a few steps before collapsing. Occasionally she would even try to run, which meant immediate contagious laughter, followed promptly with a thud and often tears. But at this point she could not be dissuaded; she was determined.

I remember one specific day I heard her giggling in her room as she ran. As I walked into the room, a photo on her bedroom wall caught my gaze. It was the only picture I had ever taken with Kinley's birth mother. It was at the baby shower our families had thrown before Kinley was born. Lindsay was glowing with her baby bump prominently protruding under her dress. I thought, *Well, now's as good a time as any to explain this to her.* I never wanted to have to sit Kinley down and have "the talk." I always wanted her to know who she was and where she came from and it was going to start today. I had no expectations. I mean who talks to their 18 month old and expects any real amount of understanding? So I grabbed the little giggling girl as she waddled past me, and I showed her the picture and said something very unceremonious. "So you know how Reesy came out of mommy's belly? Well, YOU came out of Lala's belly!"

She paused. She looked at me, then looked at the picture, then at me and then again at the picture. What I would have given to know what was going on in that head of hers. Then all of a sudden, she starts clapping and yells, "YAY! Lala's belly!!"

Tears immediately filled my eyes. She quickly wiggled down out of my arms and toddled out of the room yelling over and over again, "YAY! Lala's belly! Lala's belly!" In fact, she said it all day long. For months you could ask her whose belly she came out of and anyone who wanted could see her eyes beam with pride as she happily proclaimed where she came from. I could ask for nothing more in that moment. This was what I had prayed for; there was no fear, no confusion. She was proud of where she came from, and she would always know the truth. She came from her Lala. Whatever anxiety I still had left subsided. God was already preparing this baby's heart to not only accept her story, but to wear it with honor and to shout it from the rooftops. Her story is different than most, but it is HER story and I want her to have pride in who she is and *whose* she is.

Kinley Grows Up

Kinley has since started school. Her joyful exuberance multiplies by being constantly surrounded by her friends. School has provided a multitude of new experiences that serve to develop completely different pieces of her personality. The growth is astonishing. I've seen this tiny peanut become a firecracker. She loves to love on her friends. By the age of five, she understood one of the most important lessons I feel someone could ever learn, people matter.

The mother of a girl in Kinley's class stopped me one day out of the blue and explained that her child was having trouble adjusting to school. But every time her daughter would begin to cry, Kinley would be right there close by, comforting her. When I asked Kinley about it, without hesitating she said, "Momma, I did it because it was the right thing to do." At five years old, she made the choice to sit with her friend on the bench while everyone else played at recess. To this day, the heart of this sweet, sensitive child never ceases to amaze me. Her love for others convicts me and makes me want to be a better person.

As I began to write my piece for this book, I sat Kinley down and told her about the project we were working on. I wanted her to understand the importance of the story God had given her. I also wanted her to understand the heart behind why we would all choose to be so open about our experiences. She looked at me very intently as I shared with her, nodding her head as I explained. When I was finished she paused and then said, "Well, I guess I need to write my own part of the story too." That's my girl. I hope she follows through with that one day so she can fill in the pieces of how God's plan unfolded for her. But for the time being, she just settled for drawing you a picture of her. (See photo section.)

Eternally Grateful

I just stare at this little girl from time to time, trying to imagine our lives without her and I just can't. I can't fathom the void that would have remained had this ball of joy never entered our lives. The fact that God so perfectly orchestrated her life amazes me. He knit this precious baby together in someone else's womb, using someone else's DNA, but He meant her just for us. It was no accident that she ended up with Jeff and me; we were always meant to be her family. God was gracious enough to let me be her momma. I don't know why I am the one He blessed so much, but I am eternally grateful for His gift and for the trust He placed in me to do my job well.

A FATHER'S HEART

by Brad Pepin, Lindsay's Dad

From birth, my wife Scarlet and I prayed for our three daughters almost daily that God's purpose for their lives would be fulfilled in them and through them. With great love and a sense of "calling," we took on parenting with vigilance, pride, and focus. We were leaders, bound and determined that nothing would come between them and their destiny.

My wife and I read books, attended parenting classes at church, and enjoyed comparing notes with other parents on how to raise kids to become responsible and productive adults. We spoke Jeremiah 29:11 over them: "'For I know the plans I have for you,' declares the Lord, 'plans to prosper you and not to harm you, plans to give you hope and a future.'"

As a father of young daughters, it was my job and God-given duty to provide and protect; to guard their hearts, minds, and spirits. I took pride and enjoyed my involvement and caregiving to my kids. I saw every first footstep they made, built forts and playhouses outside, attended their school plays and music programs, often met them for lunch in the school cafeteria, and took them camping, biking, and boating. Nightly routines consisted of baths, prayers, and tuck-ins that had their own humorous endings or intimate talks. I loved being a dad of daughters; it was a privilege and a God-given blessing to steward, love, and nurture them; to fan the flame of their gifts, talents, and abilities.

As my daughters became teenagers, I would consistently encourage the girls to strive to be their best and honor God with their character, integrity, and example to their peers. I would preach that staying under God's "umbrella" would keep them safe, protected, and ease the pain during the storms of life. Getting out from under God's protection or umbrella would only bring heartache and unwanted results. My daughters could quote their mother and me saying, "The enemy (Satan) wants to kill, steal, and destroy—he doesn't play fair."

What do you do when the unexpected happens in life? Sometimes the unexpected is with one of your children. What if it's a disappointment with your wife or husband, or a close friend or loved one? How do you reconcile the difference between your hopes and desires for yourself or someone else versus the reality of the uncontrollable free will of another person or the failure of an expectation? How do you handle a curve ball in life that you don't feel prepared for, nor did you invite it into your world?

As you have read about our story, you may have related to the feeling of unexpected situations or events in your life. It might be an unexpected divorce, medical issue, financial failure, or situation that brings you to your knees. You may have had a child who commits suicide, has a drug addiction, or currently is in prison. Whatever the curve ball may be, there's a longing in each of us to be rescued. Rescued from the pain, the torment, the hurt, and the disappointment. Rescued by a Savior. Can I suggest that the only answer is to be rescued by THE Savior, Jesus?

Joy Will Come is a story of how life can be messy sometimes when the unexpected becomes your reality. The curve ball in my daughter's life instantly became a curve ball for our entire family. My role as her protector, provider, father and daddy was instantly changed in ways that I didn't anticipate. I was knocked back on my heels, wondering, "How did we get here? What could I have done differently? What were the blind spots, and how could we have prevented this?"

Joy Will Come is also a story about a redeeming God. A Father, Creator, Redeemer, and Savior who will never leave us nor forsake us. A Redeemer who always turns things around and provides a blessing and a gift on the other side of the dark valley that you may walk at some point in your life.

The heart of our Father God and why He sent His Son Jesus to die on the cross was to give us the grace needed to absorb and cover the mistakes and mishaps in our lives. The blood of Jesus is the answer to reduce and eliminate the friction and heat that our lives sometimes produce. We are flawed and broken people who need the Savior. The grace of the Father is unconditional love. Jesus suffered greatly and died on the cross so that we may be righteous in God's eyes and forgiven of our mistakes and sins. From that understanding, we are able to honor God with our lives and serve Him while He works out the flaws, wrinkles, and tarnished parts of our humanness.

As an earthly father, I was flawed. My parenting approach was text-book in many ways, and I applied the "formula"; yet it had the smell of performance and perfection. Call it fear of man and fear of failure, I was determined to have a successful and thriving family in the eyes of my peers, extended family, church community, and anyone else who was peering into our glass house. Ultimately, this trickled into my relationship with my wife and kids. At times, what was received and embedded in the hearts of my children was, "Don't make a mistake. Be good. Don't mess up. Don't disappoint your parents after all we've poured into you."

It's interesting that as parents or guardians, you want the very best for your children. But there's a fine line separating accountability, obedience, and greatness versus perfection and performance. The "grease" that must be inserted in the middle is GRACE. My own mistakes and sins were rarely used as teaching tools of humility, honesty, vulnerability, and surrender to God's lovingkindness. When my kids made mistakes and poor judgments, many times the consequence or correction sent the unintended message into their hearts of "be perfect and don't make a mistake." Yet that was not my heart as their father, nor is it the heart of our Heavenly Father; His heart is one of compassion, grace, and mercy. His lovingkindness is endless and immeasurable. If I had a "do over" as a father, I would be quick to point out the mistake, sin, mess up, and error that my children made ... coupled with more grace-filled, uncompromising, unconditional love that would bring them closer to the heart of their Heavenly Father. They would know that what they did was wrong, but because they are human, there's no way to be perfect, just forgiven. Only God is perfect. It's His kindness that leads us to repentance. No fear of man, no surrender to performance. We have an audience of one—the loving Father God.

No matter what you've done or mistakes you've made, there are none that can't be covered by the blood of Jesus. He paid a huge price on the cross for the forgiveness of our sins and the establishment of His blood covenant. As this book emphasizes, there are simple steps that we can take to find healing:

1. **Take responsibility.** Own our messy stuff and don't blame others.

    - Galatians 6:4-5: "Each one should test their own actions. Then they can take pride in themselves alone, without comparing themselves to someone else, for each one should carry their own load."

    - Proverbs 28:13: "Whoever conceals their sins does not prosper, but the one who confesses and renounces them finds mercy."

2. **Repent to God and ask for forgiveness.** Turn from the sin or mistake; make a change.

- Romans 10:9-10: "If you declare with your mouth, 'Jesus is Lord,' and believe in your heart that God raised him from the dead, you will be saved. For it is with your heart that you believe and are justified, and it is with your mouth that you profess your faith and are saved."

- 1 John 1:9: "If we confess our sins, he is faithful and just and will forgive us our sins and purify us from all unrighteousness."

3. **Accept forgiveness**—Take in God's love and forgive yourself, just as Christ has forgiven you. Your sin is now as far away as the east is from the west.

- Psalm 103:11-12: "For as high as the heavens are above the earth, so great is his love for those who fear him; as far as the east is from the west, so far has he removed our transgressions from us."

4. **Receive the Father's grace.** We can't earn grace; it's a gift from God. His love is unconditional and not earned by our performance or trying to be perfect in His eyes.

- Romans 3:22-24: "This righteousness is given through faith in Jesus Christ to all who believe. There is no difference between Jew and Gentile, for all have sinned and fall short of the glory of God, and all are justified freely by his grace through the redemption that came by Christ Jesus."

- Ephesians 2:8-9: "For it is by grace you have been saved, through faith—and this is not from yourselves, it is the gift of God—not by works, so that no one can boast."

5. **Build your faith by reading the Word of God (Bible), and get plugged into a local church.** Find a body of believers who won't judge you but will help you build your faith stronger each day.

   - Psalm 92:12-15 NKJV: "Those who are planted in the house of the Lord shall flourish in the courts of our God. They shall still bear fruit in old age; they shall be fresh and flourishing, to declare that the Lord is upright; He is my rock, and there is no unrighteousness in Him."

6. **Live in complete joy, peace, and redemption that is yours to possess.** The Holy Spirit inside of us will provide abundant peace and joy, because we serve a redeeming God.

   - Romans 15:13: "May the God of hope fill you with all joy and peace as you trust in him, so that you may overflow with hope by the power of the Holy Spirit."
   - Colossians 3:15: "Let the peace of Christ rule in your hearts, since as members of one body you were called to peace. And be thankful."

As you have read this book, my hope is that you will come to know the true heart of God as our Father, a Father's love that is unconditional and void of the repulsive spirit of fear, performance, and perfection. In our weakness, He is strong. In our failures, He is REDEMPTION. In our disappointments, He gives beauty for ashes. He simply asks us to choose His ways that are higher than our ways.

—Brad Pepin
Scarlet's husband and proud daddy of Alyssa, Lindsay, and Gabrielle

POSTSCRIPT

This is our view of the experience of an unplanned pregnancy from the perspectives of the birth mother, her mother, and her aunt who adopted the baby girl. As the narrative reveals, the birth father was present and supportive throughout the pregnancy, and he and his family remain in close, affectionate contact with the child.

CONTACT INFORMATION

Visit **scarletpepin.com** for encouraging
words sent straight to you.

Interested in having Lindsay, Bethany, and Scarlet
speak at your next event? Contact us via the
scarletpepin.com website. We would love to meet you.

Check out Lindsay's website:
Lindsaypepinophus.com

Connect with Bethany at her blog:
Blessmymessblog.blogspot.com

Connect on Instagram:
@lindsayophus
@scarlet.pepin
@blessmymessblog

A *Brad, Alyssa, Lindsay, Scarlet, and Gabrielle at Lindsay's high school graduation. Lindsay is 6 months pregnant.*

B *Brad, Lindsay, and Scarlet on prom night. Lindsay is 5 months pregnant.*

C *Lindsay is 9 months pregnant. Reese is touching her future baby sister.*

D *Lindsay holding baby Reese with Bethany. Lindsay is 8 months pregnant.*

E *Scarlet, Mimi, holding one day old Kinley at Reese's first birthday.*

F *Kinley is born! August 11th 2012.*
G *Cake given to Jeff and Bethany asking them to be Baby Girl's parents.*
H *Jeff and Bethany with their new baby, Kinley.*
I *Kinley's picture of adoption, showing Bethany holding her as a baby.*
J *Kinley's official adoption day!*
K *Malachi and Lindsay's wedding with flower girl Kinley.*

L *Mimi and Pops with their three granddaughters, Reese, Gentry, and Kinley.*

M *Kinley 6 months old.*

N *Kinley at age 3.*

O *Kinley at age 3.*

P *Kinley at age 2 with her Lala (Lindsay).*

Q *Mimi and Kinley at the fair.*

R *Mimi and Kinley flying to New Orleans to see Lindsay.*

S *Jeff and Bethany with Reese, Kinley, and Gentry.*
T *Kinley with her mom, Bethany.*
U *Kinley with her dad, Jeff.*

V *Kinley at age 4 with Lindsay.*
W *Kinley at age 6.*
X *Kinley with her two sisters, Reese and Gentry.*

Made in the USA
Las Vegas, NV
31 August 2021